How to use your *Flip Quiz*

If you are answering questions on your own, just cover the answers with your hand or a piece of card. You may want to write down your answers and count up your scores for each quiz.

If you are doing the quizzes with a partner or in teams, unfold the base and stand the *Flip Quiz* on a flat surface between you and your partner. Read aloud the questions (but not the answers!) and allow your partner to say the answers or write them down.

You may answer each question in turn or answer an entire quiz in turn. Keep your scores on a piece of paper and compare results.

The illustrations are there to help you get the right answers when competing with a partner. For instance, if you are answering Quiz 1 questions, you will be looking at and reading out Quiz 2. However, the images you will see are clues to help you with Quiz 1. The labels next to the illustrations tell you which question they are clues for.

Some questions are about specific sports, and there are plenty of general sports questions to suit everyone.

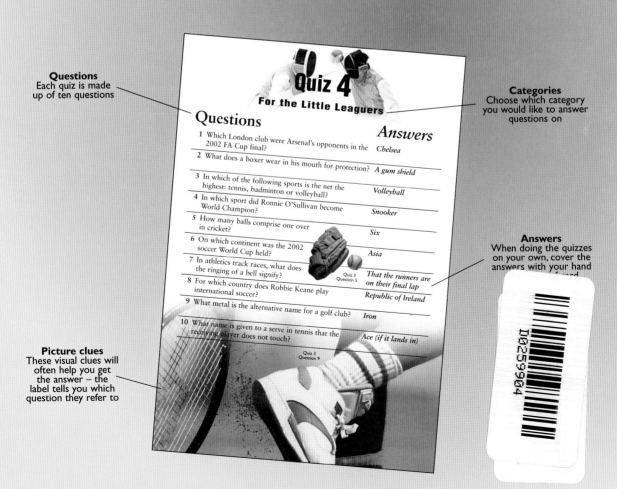

Questions
Each quiz is made up of ten questions

Categories
Choose which category you would like to answer questions on

Answers
When doing the quizzes on your own, cover the answers with your hand or a piece of card

Picture clues
These visual clues will often help you get the answer – the label tells you which question they refer to

Quiz 4
For the Little Leaguers

Questions   **Answers**

1 Which London club were Arsenal's opponents in the 2002 FA Cup final?   *Chelsea*

2 What does a boxer wear in his mouth for protection?   *A gum shield*

3 In which of the following sports is the net the highest: tennis, badminton or volleyball?   *Volleyball*

4 In which sport did Ronnie O'Sullivan become World Champion?   *Snooker*

5 How many balls comprise one over in cricket?   *Six*

6 On which continent was the 2002 soccer World Cup held?   *Asia*

7 In athletics track races, what does the ringing of a bell signify?   *That the runners are on their final lap*

Quiz 3 Question 5

8 For which country does Robbie Keane play international soccer?   *Republic of Ireland*

9 What metal is the alternative name for a golf club?   *Iron*

10 What name is given to a serve in tennis that the receiving player does not touch?   *Ace (if it lands in)*

Quiz 3 Question 9

Questions	Answers
1 Which Australian city is to host the 2006 Commonwealth Games?	*Melbourne*
2 Which sport is played by the Sheffield Sharks?	*Basketball*
3 What is the last event in a decathlon?	*1500 m*
4 Who was sent home from Ireland's World Cup squad in May 2002 after a dispute with the manager?	*Roy Keane*
5 Which county joined the Cricket County Championship in 1992?	*Durham*
6 Was Michael Owen born in York, Liverpool or Chester?	*Chester*
7 What nationality is the England manager Sven Goran Eriksson?	*Swedish*
8 Which Scottish driver won the Monaco Grand Prix in May 2002?	*David Coulthard*
9 Which legendary tennis star's statue was unveiled at Wimbledon in 1984?	*Fred Perry*
10 Which was the first London club to win the Football League Championship?	*Arsenal*

Quiz I
Question 10

Quiz I
Question 6

Quiz 1
A Sports Bag

Questions	Answers
1 In rowing, what is the name of Cambridge University's reserve team?	*"Goldie"*
2 Which Frenchman was the first Formula One driver to register 50 Grand Prix wins?	*Alain Prost*
3 What is the first event in a decathlon?	*100 m*
4 Which Liverpool midfielder hobbled out of England's World Cup squad in May 2002 after breaking a bone?	*Danny Murphy*
5 Which member of the Royal Family officially closed the 2006 Commonwealth Games?	*Prince Edward*
6 What is the only ball sport that is governed by the ASA?	*Water polo*
7 Was David Beckham born in London, Birmingham or Manchester?	*London*
8 Which country hosted the 2002 Winter Olympics?	*The United States*
9 Which goalkeeper was England's most capped footballer in the 20th century?	*Peter Shilton*
10 In 1991, who broke Bob Beamon's 23-year-old world long jump record?	*Mike Powell*

Quiz 2
Question 7

Quiz 2
Question 9

Quiz 4
For the Little Leaguers

Questions	Answers
1 Which London club were Arsenal's opponents in the 2002 FA Cup final?	Chelsea
2 What does a boxer wear in his mouth for protection?	A gum shield
3 In which of the following sports is the net the highest: tennis, badminton or volleyball?	Volleyball
4 In which sport did Ronnie O'Sullivan become World Champion?	Snooker
5 How many balls comprise one over in cricket?	Six
6 On which continent was the 2002 soccer World Cup held?	Asia
7 In athletics track races, what does the ringing of a bell signify?	That the runners are on their final lap
8 For which country does Robbie Keane play international soccer?	Republic of Ireland
9 What metal is the alternative name for a golf club?	Iron
10 What name is given to a serve in tennis that the receiving player does not touch?	Ace (if it lands in)

Quiz 3
Question 5

Quiz 3
Question 9

Questions	Answers
1 Which soccer team does the Spice Girl Mel C support?	*Liverpool*
2 What is a golf bunker filled with?	*Sand*
3 What does a boxer's trainer throw into the ring if his fighter is taking too much punishment?	*The towel*
4 In which sport can a foil or sabre be used?	*Fencing*
5 What sport is played by the New York Yankees?	*Baseball*
6 Which country does Fabian Barthez play international soccer for?	*France*
7 How many laps of the track are run in an outdoor 400 m race?	*One*
8 On a dartboard, which has the largest area: a bullseye, a double or a treble?	*The double*
9 In which game is the term love used?	*Tennis*
10 In cricket, how many runs are scored for a shot that hits the ground before passing the boundary?	*Four*

Quiz 4
Question 3

Quiz 6
Martial Art Mania

Questions	Answers
1 Which martial art made its Olympic debut at the 2000 Sydney Games?	*Taekwando*
2 What name is given to a grade in judo?	*A dan (once at black belt)*
3 In which 1984 film did Ralph Maccio play a teenage martial arts exponent?	**The Karate Kid**
4 In judo which part of the leg is referred to as the *hiza*?	*Knee*
5 What was the name of the martial arts warriors that originated in 9th century Japan?	*Ninjas*
6 In kendo, where on the body are the *kote* worn: the feet, the hands or the head?	***The hands, they are protective gauntlets***
7 In which sport is the referee called a *Gyoji*?	***Sumo wrestling***
8 What does *jujitsu* mean when translated into English?	***The gentle way***
9 What three-letter word is the name given to the belt that ties a judo uniform?	**Obi**
10 In which country did *taekwando* originate?	*Korea*

Quiz 5
Question 8

Quiz 5
Question 4

Quiz 5
Martial Art Mania

Questions	Answers
1 What are the swords made from that are used in the sport kendo?	*Bamboo*
2 In which city was judo founded?	*Tokyo*
3 In sumo wrestling, what is the *mawashi*?	*The loincloth worn by wrestlers*
4 Which martial arts hero, who died in 1973, starred in the film *Enter The Dragon*?	*Bruce Lee*
5 What does the word karate mean when translated into English?	*Empty hand*
6 Which of the following is not a style of kung fu: White Crane, Flying Fish, Lama Pai?	*Flying Fish*
7 On which soccer ground did Eric Cantona launch a kung fu assault on a spectator?	*Selhurst Park*
8 What name was given to the martial arts soldiers first employed in Japan as palace guards?	*Samurai*
9 In which martial art is the attacker known as the *Uke* and the one receiving the attack the *Nage*?	*Aikido*
10 In a judo contest what is the *tatami*?	*The mat on which the contest is fought*

Quiz 6
Question 7

Quiz 8
A Sports Bag

Questions	Answers
1 In 1998, Sweden beat Finland 1-0 in the final of which World Championships. At which sport?	*Ice hockey*
2 What do the letters PB next to an athlete's time indicate?	*Personal best*
3 Which was the first British city to host the Commonwealth Games twice?	*Edinburgh*
4 Which grade follows a yellow belt in judo?	*An orange belt*
5 At which Scottish golf venue are the Eden Course and the Jubilee Course?	*St. Andrews*
6 How many consecutive Wimbledon titles did Bjorn Borg win?	*Five*
7 In 1994, which West Indian batsman scored 501 not out in one innings?	*Brian Lara*
8 In which decade was soccer's World Cup first contested?	*1930s, the first in 1930*
9 Which golfer wrote a controversial book in 2000 entitled *Into The Bear Pit*?	*Mark James*
10 In which city is the Dutch soccer club, Feyenoord, based?	*Rotterdam*

Quiz 7
Question 6

Quiz 7
A Sports Bag

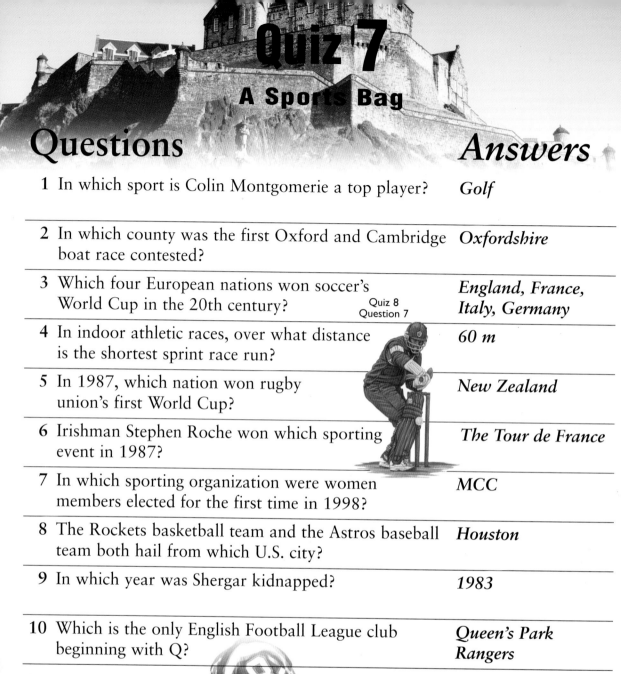

Questions	Answers
1 In which sport is Colin Montgomerie a top player?	*Golf*
2 In which county was the first Oxford and Cambridge boat race contested?	*Oxfordshire*
3 Which four European nations won soccer's World Cup in the 20th century?	*England, France, Italy, Germany*
4 In indoor athletic races, over what distance is the shortest sprint race run?	*60 m*
5 In 1987, which nation won rugby union's first World Cup?	*New Zealand*
6 Irishman Stephen Roche won which sporting event in 1987?	*The Tour de France*
7 In which sporting organization were women members elected for the first time in 1998?	*MCC*
8 The Rockets basketball team and the Astros baseball team both hail from which U.S. city?	*Houston*
9 In which year was Shergar kidnapped?	*1983*
10 Which is the only English Football League club beginning with Q?	*Queen's Park Rangers*

Quiz 8
Question 7

Quiz 8
Question 1

Quiz 10
A Sports Bag

Questions	Answers
1 Which U.S. heavyweight boxer is nicknamed "The Real Deal"?	*Evander Holyfield*
2 What do the initials UR stand for in horse racing?	*Unseated rider*
3 Which footballer replaced Lady Diana in the international campaign against landmines?	*David Ginola*
4 How many hoops are used in the game of croquet: 6, 8 or 10?	*6*
5 Which tennis star won her first Wimbledon Singles title in 1974?	*Chris Evert*
6 At which venue did Muhammed Ali light the Olympic flame?	*Atlanta*
7 Europe, Soling, Finn and Tornado are all Olympic classes in which event?	*Yachting*
8 The Spanish side Real Madrid won the first ever European Cup. What does Real mean in English?	*Royal*
9 In which sport is shortstop a fielding position?	*Baseball*
10 In which sport did Heather McKay win the World Championship for 16 consecutive years?	*Squash*

Quiz 9
Question 8

Quiz 9
Question 2

Quiz 9
A Sports Bag

Questions	Answers
1 Which country won the most gold medals at the 2000 Sydney Olympics?	*The United States*
2 In which board game will you find a Queen's bishop?	*Chess*
3 How many players are there in a Gaelic football team: 11, 13 or 15?	*15*
4 What nickname is given to tennis player Martina Hingis?	*"The Swiss Miss"*
5 Which country is to host the 2008 Summer Olympics?	*China*
6 What title provides the nickname of the boxer Naseem Hamed?	*"Prince"*
7 What is the name of the Scottish winter sports venue in the Cairngorm Mountains?	*Aviemore*
8 Freestyle and Greco-Roman are both styles of what?	*Wrestling*
9 In which city is the headquarters of British athletics?	*Birmingham*
10 In which sport did Ballyregan Bob win 32 consecutive races?	*Greyhound racing*

Quiz 10
Question 1

Questions	Answers
1 Lincoln, East End, Manchester and London are all types of what?	*All types of dartboard*
2 Which sport can be contested over a Hereford round and a York round?	*Archery*
3 Which sport combines cross country skiing and rifle shooting?	*The biathlon*
4 In which game are projectiles thrown at stakes called hobs?	*Quoits*
5 Which actor was elected President of the National Rifle Association at a 1998 meeting in Philadelphia?	*Charlton Heston*
6 Who acquired the nickname of "The Crafty Cockney"?	*Eric Bristow*
7 In which Surrey town is the British National Shooting Centre?	*Bisley*
8 Which number is directly opposite number 20 on a dartboard?	*Three*
9 Which shooting season begins on August 12th and is known as "the Glorious Twelfth"?	*Grouse shooting*
10 Which boy's name is also the name of the target ball in crown green bowls?	*Jack*

Quiz 11
Question 6

Quiz 11
Question 10

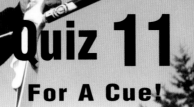

Quiz 11
For A Cue!

Questions	Answers
1 How many points is the yellow ball worth in snooker?	*Two*
2 Straight, eight ball and nine ball are all varieties of which game?	*Pool*
3 Who was crowned snooker World Champion for the first time in 2002?	*Peter Ebdon*
4 In billiards, how many points are awarded for potting the red?	*Three*
5 At which Sheffield venue are the Embassy Snooker World Championships held?	*The Crucible*
6 What nationality is former snooker World Champion Cliff Thorburn?	*Canadian*
7 How many points are awarded to the opponent for a foul stroke in billiards?	*Two*
8 Which Welshman won the last of his six world snooker titles in 1978?	*Ray Reardon*
9 In which film did Paul Newman first play the pool player Fast Eddie Felson?	The Hustler
10 Who won his first world snooker title in 1990 and his seventh in 1999?	*Stephen Hendry*

Quiz 12
Question 5

Quiz 12
Question 9

Questions	Answers
1 In the 1970s, who became the first Brazilian driver to be crowned Formula One World Champion?	*Emerson Fittipaldi*
2 In America what name is given to a bunker in the game of golf?	*Sand trap*
3 Which American football team are known as the Falcons?	*Atlanta*
4 What name is given to the electronic eye used at Wimbledon tennis tournaments?	*Cyclops*
5 Which baseball team's stadium is known as The House That Ruth Built?	*New York Yankees*
6 Which Moroccan athlete became the first man to run 5000 m in under 13 minutes?	*Said Aouita*
7 Who caused a major upset in the world of boxing in 1990 when he beat Mike Tyson?	*James "Buster" Douglas*
8 What name is given to cycling contests in which the riders start on opposite sides of the track?	*Pursuit*
9 Which sport is played by the Philadelphia Flyers?	*Ice hockey*
10 Which Scottish golfer was captain of Europe's 2002 Ryder Cup team?	*Sam Torrance*

Quiz 13
Question 3

Quiz 13
Question 9

Quiz 13
A Sports Bag

Questions	Answers
1 Crouch roll and poke fall are both types of what?	*Styles of diving*
2 Which country does the athlete Merlene Ottey represent?	*Jamaica*
3 Which bird provides the name of the United States' rugby union team?	*The Eagles*
4 How many minutes is a golfer allowed to search for a lost ball?	*Five minutes*
5 Which American football team are called the Bengals?	*Cincinnati*
6 In boxing, what name is given to an illegal punch to the back of the head?	*A rabbit punch*
7 Which sporting trophy was held by the United States for 132 years?	*The America's Cup (in yachting)*
8 Which Scandinavian city hosted the World Athletics Championships in 1995?	*Gothenburg*
9 Which British driver was Formula One World Champion in 1996?	*Damon Hill*
10 Which country jointly hosted the 2000 European Football Championships with the Netherlands?	*Belgium*

Quiz 14
Question 5

Quiz 16
A Sports Bag

Questions	Answers
1 How many red balls are on a snooker table at the start of play?	*15*
2 In horse racing, why was the 2001 Cheltenham Festival called off?	*The outbreak of foot and mouth disease*
3 What name is given to the handles on a gymnastic horse?	*Pommels*
4 Which race takes place over a distance of 42.195 km?	*Marathon*
5 In which sport were Denmark World Champions from 1983 to 1988: speedway, orienteering or hockey?	*Speedway*
6 In which country is the Monza motor racing circuit?	*Italy*
7 Who was the World Heavyweight Boxing Champion from 1937 to 1949?	*Joe Louis*
8 Which London airport staged the Grand National during World War I?	*Gatwick*
9 In October 2005, the horse Hurricane Run won which prestigious race?	*Prix de l'Arc de Triomphe*
10 Which 18-a-side ball sport was devised by an Australian called George Ligowsky?	*Australian rules football*

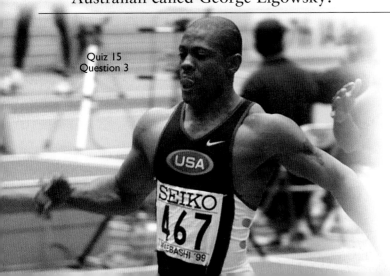

Quiz 15
Question 3

Quiz 15
Question 1

Quiz 15
A Sports Bag

Questions	Answers
1 At the Aqueduct in New York, would you be watching baseball, horse racing or swimming?	*Horse racing*
2 In which sport is the net 91 cm high in the middle?	*Tennis*
3 Which U.S. sprinter set a world record for the 100 m in 1999?	*Maurice Greene*
4 What is the table bed of a snooker table made from?	*Slate*
5 Which Irish boxer was nicknamed "The Clones Cyclone"?	*Barry McGuigan*
6 In which country is Turnberry Golf Course?	*Scotland*
7 In horse racing, what were used for the first time at Newmarket in July 1965?	*Starting stalls*
8 Which Australian tennis star won the most men's singles titles at Wimbledon in the 1960s?	*Rod Laver*
9 Which soccer club won the European Champions Cup in 2002?	*Real Madrid*
10 What was the unusual result of the 1877 Oxford and Cambridge boat race?	*It was a dead heat*

Quiz 16
Question 7

Quiz 18
An Olympic Odyssey

Questions	Answers
1 Which British athlete won a heptathlon gold medal at the 2000 Olympics?	*Denise Lewis*
2 Which is the most highly populated city to have hosted the Olympic games?	*Tokyo*
3 Over what distance did British athlete Roger Black win an Olympic silver medal in 1996?	*400 m*
4 Which Asian country competed in the Summer Olympics in 1984, the first time they had entered since 1952?	*China*
5 Which is the highest city to have hosted the Summer Olympics?	*Mexico City*
6 The five Olympic rings are black, red, blue, yellow and what?	*Green*
7 Which javelin thrower won Britain's only track and field gold at the 1984 Olympics?	*Tessa Sanderson*
8 In which country is Lillehammer, the venue for the 1994 Winter Olympics?	*Norway*
9 Which American won seven gold medals at the 1972 games?	*Mark Spitz*
10 In which decade were the modern Summer Olympics first staged?	*1890s (the first in 1896 in Athens)*

Quiz 17
Question 9

Quiz 17
Question 2

Quiz 17

An Olympic Odyssey

	Questions	Answers
1	Which cyclist won Great Britain's first gold medal at the 2000 Sydney Olympics?	*Jason Queally*
2	How are the five major continents represented on the Olympic flag?	*By five interlocking rings*
3	Which was the first city outside of Europe to host the Summer Olympics?	*St. Louis*
4	Who won a gold medal for Great Britain at the 2000 Olympics with a jump that measured 17.71 m?	*Jonathan Edwards*
5	In which country is Nagano, the venue for the 1998 Winter Olympics?	*Japan*
6	Which country's athletes traditionally lead the parade at the opening ceremony of the Summer Olympics?	*Greece*
7	In which year did the United States boycott the Moscow Olympics?	*1980*
8	What do the initials IOC stand for?	*International Olympic Committee*
9	At which team sport did Britain win an Olympic gold medal in 1988?	*Hockey*
10	Which was the first city in the Southern Hemisphere to host the Summer Olympics?	*Melbourne*

Quiz 18
Question 9

Quiz 18
Question 5

Quiz 20
A Sports Bag

Questions	Answers
1 Which was the first German city to host the Olympic games?	Berlin
2 In the United States what do the initials NFC stand for?	National Football Conference
3 Which sport was originally called sphairistike?	Tennis
4 For which country does Edgar Davids play international soccer?	Holland
5 In which sport would the Detroit Tigers face the Chicago Cubs?	Baseball
6 In 2001, which U.S. athlete held the world records for the 200 m, 300 m and 400 m?	Michael Johnson
7 Which country hosts The Monte Carlo Grand Prix?	Monaco
8 What is the first event in a heptathlon?	100 m hurdles
9 Which English soccer team left Burnden Park to move to the Reebok Stadium?	Bolton Wanderers
10 Which country won soccer's European Nations Championships in 2000?	France

Quiz 19
Question 5

Quiz 19
A Sports Bag

Questions	Answers
1 In which team sport does Great Britain play the United States for the Westchester Cup?	*Polo*
2 In which city is the Hungarian Grand Prix held?	*Budapest*
3 Which country does Gabriel Batistuta play international soccer for?	*Argentina*
4 What sport would you be watching if the Somerset Sabres were facing the Sussex Sharks?	*Cricket*
5 Which sporting projectile, for male athletes, weighs 2 kg and is thrown from a 2.5 m circle?	*The discus*
6 Which is the only country to win three European Nations Championships at soccer?	*Germany*
7 What is the last event in a heptathlon?	*800 m*
8 Which was the only team to win the Super Bowl three times in the 1990s?	*Dallas Cowboys*
9 In 2002, which soccer club played their last home game at Craven Cottage prior to its renovation?	*Fulham*
10 Which city was to host the 1944 Olympics, which were cancelled due to World War II?	*London*

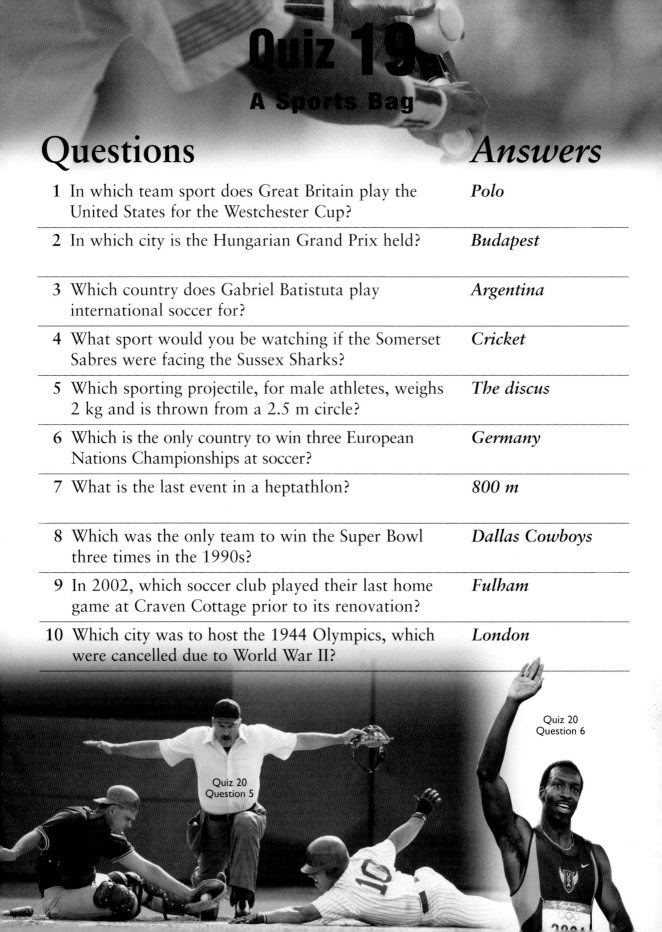

Quiz 20
Question 6

Quiz 20
Question 5

Quiz 22
A Sports Bag

Questions	Answers
1 Who was the first cricketer to score 5000 runs, take 350 wickets and 100 catches in test cricket?	*Ian Botham*
2 Which country does Jennifer Capriati represent at tennis?	*The United States*
3 In golf, what name is given to the area of short grass between the fairway and the approach to the green?	*The apron*
4 What would one be playing if achieving a turkey between the bedposts?	*Ten pin bowling*
5 Who was Steve Redgrave's rowing partner when he won a gold medal at the 1988 Olympics?	*Andy Holmes*
6 Which Brazilian was voted World Footballer of the Year in 1999?	*Rivaldo*
7 What did the crown green bowler David Bryant usually have in his mouth when he was playing?	*A pipe*
8 On a dartboard which number lies between 9 and 5?	*12*
9 Why do American footballers paint black marks across their cheeks?	*As protection against the sun's glare*
10 Camogie is the women's version of which sport, popular in Ireland?	*Hurling*

Quiz 21
Question 10

Quiz 21
Question 7

Quiz 21
A Sports Bag

Questions	Answers
1 In which sport was Clive Woodward appointed the manager of England's international team?	*Rugby Union*
2 At which Premiership soccer ground is the Matthew Harding Stand?	*Stamford Bridge*
3 In baseball, what is the equivalent of a cricket bowler?	*The pitcher*
4 What nationality is Liverpool midfielder Patrick Berger?	*Czech*
5 At what game did Gary Kasparov become World Champion?	*Chess*
6 How many Wimbledon singles titles did John McEnroe win?	*Three*
7 Which French footballer was voted PFA Player of the Year in 1999?	*David Ginola*
8 Which sport is played by the Chicago Bulls?	*Basketball*
9 In which twelve-a-side team game do the players use a stick called a caman?	*Shinty*
10 Which nation won the 1992 European Football Championships?	*Denmark*

Quiz 22
Question 7

Quiz 22
Question 6

Quiz 24

The Cold Facts!!!

Questions	Answers
1 Which Austrian skier won four World Downhill championships in the 1970s?	*Franz Klammer*
2 The ski resort of Zermatt stands at the foot of which Swiss mountain?	*The Matterhorn*
3 Which film, starring John Candy, told the story of the Jamaican bobsleigh team?	*Cool Runnings*
4 In downhill skiing, does a black graded piste indicate an easy or a difficult slope?	*A difficult slope*
5 What name is given to the area where an ice hockey player is sent if commiting a serious offence?	*The sin bin*
6 Which country won the most medals at the 1998 Winter Olympics: the United States, Russia or Germany?	*Germany (with 29 medals in total)*
7 In which sport do competitors soop the ice and throw stones at houses?	*Curling*
8 In which country is the Winter Olympic venue of Innsbruck?	*Austria*
9 Which sport includes events called the halfpipe, the slopestyle and the boardercross?	*Snowboarding*
10 Which is the only capital city to have hosted the Winter Olympics?	*Oslo, capital of Norway*

Quiz 23
Question 8

Quiz 23
Question 3

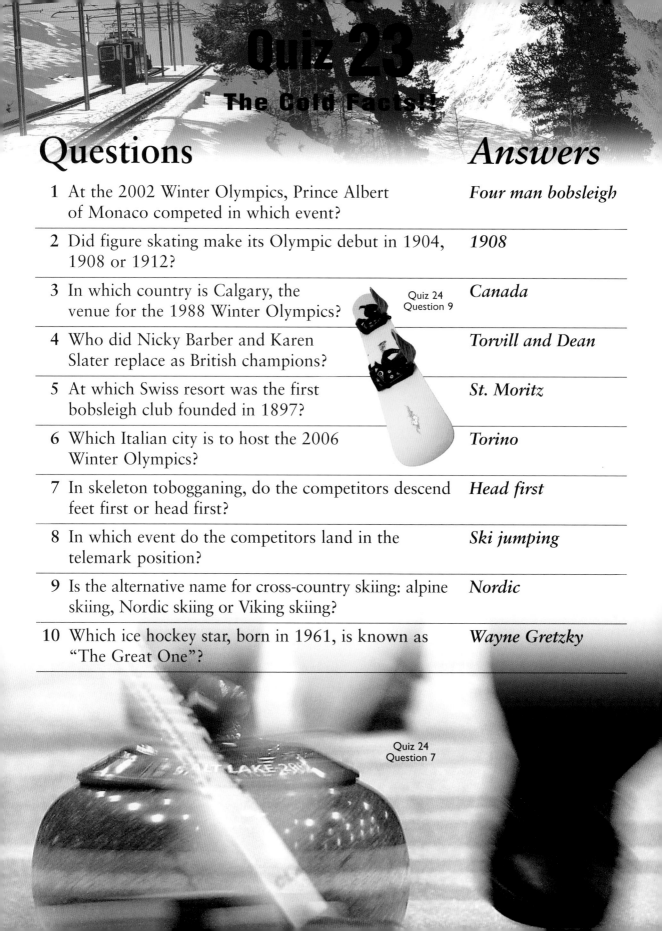

Questions

Answers

1	At the 2002 Winter Olympics, Prince Albert of Monaco competed in which event?	*Four man bobsleigh*
2	Did figure skating make its Olympic debut in 1904, 1908 or 1912?	*1908*
3	In which country is Calgary, the venue for the 1988 Winter Olympics?	*Canada*
4	Who did Nicky Barber and Karen Slater replace as British champions?	*Torvill and Dean*
5	At which Swiss resort was the first bobsleigh club founded in 1897?	*St. Moritz*
6	Which Italian city is to host the 2006 Winter Olympics?	*Torino*
7	In skeleton tobogganing, do the competitors descend feet first or head first?	*Head first*
8	In which event do the competitors land in the telemark position?	*Ski jumping*
9	Is the alternative name for cross-country skiing: alpine skiing, Nordic skiing or Viking skiing?	*Nordic*
10	Which ice hockey star, born in 1961, is known as "The Great One"?	*Wayne Gretzky*

Quiz 24
Question 9

Quiz 24
Question 7

Quiz 26
A Sports Bag

Questions	Answers
1 In 1927, the first World Championships for which indoor sport took place at Camkin's Hall, Birmingham?	*Snooker*
2 Which American football team play their home games at the Robert F. Kennedy Stadium?	*Washington Redskins*
3 With which sport do you associate Harvey Smith, Nick Skelton and Rob Hoekstra?	*Show jumping*
4 Which Scottish athlete struck gold in the 100 m at the 1980 Moscow Olympics?	*Alan Wells*
5 Which South African golfer was the only non-U.S. winner of the U.S. Open in the 1990s?	*Ernie Els*
6 Which race was first run in Massachusetts in 1897 and is now contested annually every April on Patriot's Day?	*The Boston Marathon*
7 In baseball, what name is given to the completion of a circuit of bases on one hit?	*A home run*
8 From which country do the soccer team Anderlecht hail?	*Belgium*
9 Which of the following was first held in 1911: Tour de France, Monte Carlo Rally or Fastnet Yacht Race?	*The Monte Carlo Rally*
10 Outcrop, big wall and crag are all forms of what?	*Rock climbing*

Quiz 25
Question 5

Quiz 25
Question 6

Quiz 25
A Sports Quiz

Questions	Answers
1 Which sport, involving cross country running and route finding, held its first World Championships in 1966?	*Orienteering*
2 Which German golfer won the U.S. Masters in 1993?	*Bernhard Langer*
3 Which American football team plays its home matches at Candlestick Park in California?	*San Francisco 49ers*
4 Who was disqualified after winning the men's 100 m at the 1988 Olympics?	*Ben Johnson*
5 What did the Inter Cities Fairs Cup change its name to?	*UEFA Cup*
6 Which nation did France beat 3-0 in the final of soccer's World Cup in 1998?	*Brazil*
7 What shape is the ball in Australian rules football?	*Oval*
8 From which country do the soccer team Fiorentina hail?	*Italy*
9 Which Canadian athlete won the Olympic gold medal for the Men's 100 m in 1996?	*Donovan Bailey*
10 Was the Oxford and Cambridge boat race first contested in the 18th, 19th or 20th century?	*19th century*

Quiz 26
Question 7

Quiz 28
A Record Breaking Round

Questions	Answers
1 Over what distance did the U.S. athlete Butch Reynolds hold a world record?	*400 m*
2 In 1998, who became the youngest footballer to score a hat-trick in the English Premiership?	*Michael Owen*
3 Which nation won every World Championship from 1990 to 2001 for women's ice hockey?	*Canada*
4 Which country did cricketer Javed Miandad represent?	*Pakistan*
5 Brazil was the first nation to win soccer's World Cup three times. Which country were the second?	*Italy*
6 Which baseball team won a record 37 World Series in the 20th century? Quiz 27 Question 4	*New York Yankees*
7 In 1996, which 14 year old Russian tennis star became the youngest player to win a Federation Cup match?	*Anna Kournikova*
8 Which golfer won over $9 million prize money in 2000?	*Tiger Woods*
9 Who has scored a record 11,174 cricket test runs representing Australia?	*Allan Border*
10 Who won nine Formula One Grand Prix races in 2000?	*Michael Schumacher*

Quiz 27
Question 5

Quiz 27
A Record Breaking Round

Questions	Answers
1 Which was the only soccer club to win ten FA Cup finals in the 20th century?	*Manchester United*
2 Who was the first golfer to win six U.S. Masters?	*Jack Nicklaus*
3 Which record breaking U.S. jockey was nicknamed "The Shoe"?	*Willie Shoemaker*
4 Which legendary Brazilian footballer scored a record 1,279 goals in his first class career?	*Pele*
5 Which was the first nation to win cricket's World Cup twice?	*The West Indies*
6 Which nation won the most table tennis World Championships in the 20th century?	*China*
7 Which U.S. tennis ace won 13 Grand Slam titles between 1990 and 2000?	*Pete Sampras*
8 Which European soccer club were named Team of the Century by FIFA in 1998?	*Real Madrid*
9 In 1935 which athlete, nicknamed "The Ebony Express", broke six world records in one day?	*Jesse Owens*
10 Who won a record 20 Wimbledon titles between 1961 and 1979?	*Billie Jean King*

Quiz 28
Question 3

Quiz 28
Question 7

Quiz 30
Water Wise

Questions	Answers
1 How many rowers are in each of the crews for the Oxford and Cambridge boat race?	*Eight rowers, plus one Cox per boat*
2 In the canoeing racing category, what does the letter C stand for?	*Canadian*
3 On a yacht, what are sheets?	*Ropes*
4 How many lanes does an Olympic standard swimming pool have?	*Eight*
5 In Olympic competitions, what is the height of the diving highboard?	*10 m*
6 In water polo, which player wears a red cap?	*The goalkeeper*
7 Which entrepreneur skippered a boat called *Virgin Atlantic Challenger II* when it crossed the Atlantic?	*Richard Branson*
8 In an Olympic steeplechase race, how many times is the water jump negotiated?	*Seven*
9 Which was the first nation, other than the United States, to win yachting's Americas Cup?	*Australia*
10 Which swimming stroke was introduced into competition in 1952?	*Butterfly*

Quiz 29
Question 8

Quiz 29
Water Wise

Questions	Answers
1 How many players comprise a water polo team?	*Seven*
2 When did the first Fastnet Race take place: 1895, 1925 or 1945?	*1925*
3 What is the length of an Olympic standard swimming pool?	*50 m*
4 The Leander Club is the oldest club in the U.K. in which sport?	*Rowing*
5 On which lake was Donald Campbell killed?	*Coniston Water*
6 Which Australian woman was the first to swim 100 m in under one minute?	*Dawn Fraser*
7 What does the B stand for in the acronym SCUBA?	*Breathing*
8 Which water sport can have a dock start or a beach start?	*Water skiing*
9 What B word is the name of the housing for a boat's compass?	*Binnacle*
10 How many different swimming strokes comprise a relay race in the Olympics?	*Four*

Quiz 30
Question 10

Quiz 32

For the Little Leaguers

Questions	Answers
1 How many runs are awarded for a wide in cricket?	*One*
2 Who were the beaten finalists in the 2002 soccer World Cup?	*Germany*
3 What name is given to the starting area in a Formula One Grand Prix race?	*The grid*
4 Would you expect to see John Higgins running around a track, kicking a ball or chalking a cue?	*Chalking a cue*
5 On what type of surface does the game of curling take place?	*Ice*
6 What nationality is the footballer Thierry Henry?	*French*
7 In badminton, what is the equivalent of a ball?	*Shuttlecock*
8 Where do you find a golf link course?	*By the coast*
9 Before 2002, when was the last World Cup in soccer held?	*1998*
10 In which sport has Greg Rusedski represented Britain?	*Tennis*

Quiz 31
Question 9

Quiz 31

For the Little Leaguers

Questions	Answers
1 Which sport has Nasser Hussain captained for England?	*In cricket*
2 In which race do competitors negotiate fences called The Chair and Becher's Brook?	*The Grand National*
3 In the Premiership, how many points do teams receive for winning a game?	*Three*
4 What name is given to the wooden log that is tossed in the Highland Games?	*The caber*
5 Mick McCarthy managed which international soccer side in 2002?	*The Republic of Ireland*
6 How many members of the fielding side in a cricket team are allowed to wear gloves?	*Only one (the wicket keeper)*
7 For which soccer club did Alan Shearer score his 200th Premiership goal in 2002?	*Newcastle United*
8 What is the ice hockey equivalent of a ball?	*The puck*
9 Who won the 2002 soccer World Cup?	*Brazil*
10 Would you see Jona Lomu skiing down a hill, scoring a try or throwing a punch?	*Scoring a try*

Quiz 32
Question 7

Quiz 32
Question 4

Quiz 34
A Sports Bag

Questions	Answers
1 Which sport is governed by the CPSA?	*Clay pigeon shooting*
2 What kind of animal was Miska, the official mascot of the 1980 Moscow Olympics?	*A bear*
3 Which sport is played at the U.S. venue of Flushing Meadows?	*Tennis*
4 What is the name of Lancashire's cricket test ground?	*Old Trafford*
5 In which Swiss city is the headquarters of the International Olympic Committee?	*Lausanne*
6 Which golfer is known as "The Walrus"?	*Craig Staedler*
7 How many players comprise a hockey team?	*Eleven*
8 In the 1930s, which tennis star was the last British player to win the men's singles at Wimbledon?	*Fred Perry*
9 Which member of the British royal family owns the Oval Cricket Ground?	*Prince Charles*
10 At which racket sport is the Uber Cup contested?	*Badminton*

Quiz 33
Question 9

Quiz 33

A Sports Bag

Questions	Answers
1 In which Olympic event did women first compete against men?	*Equestrianism*
2 In professional boxing, how long does the break between the rounds last?	*One minute*
3 Which sport is played by the Los Angeles Lakers?	*Basketball*
4 What was the name of Formula One star Jacques Villeneuve's father?	*Gilles Villeneuve*
5 In which year was the first modern Olympic games cancelled due to war?	*1916*
6 Which sport is played at Cowdray Park?	*Polo*
7 Which Portuguese soccer club play at home at the Stadium of Light?	*Benfica*
8 The Epsom Derby is restricted to horses of what age?	*Three year olds*
9 Which member of England's 2002 World Cup soccer squad was their most capped player?	*David Seaman*
10 How many players comprise a softball team?	*Nine*

Quiz 34
Question 10

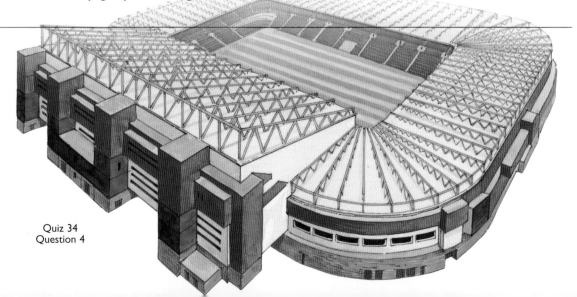

Quiz 34
Question 4

Quiz 36
Terminology Teasers

Questions	Answers
1 How many hulls does a sailing boat called a trimaran have?	*Three*
2 In which sport was the axel named after Axel Rudolph Paulser?	*Ice-skating*
3 What bird's name is given to a score of two under par in golf?	*Eagle*
4 In which sporting activity is a barani a front somersault with a half twist?	*Trampolining*
5 In which sport is the word *bonspeil* used to describe an important game?	*Curling*
6 In which sport is there a move called a crucifix?	*Men's gymnastics*
7 Which court game was formerly known as paddleball?	*Racketball*
8 What is a fencer doing if performing an *appel* during a bout?	*Stamping their feet*
9 In golf, what is a bogey?	*One over par on a hole*
10 What is ice hockey's equivalent of a kick off called?	*A face off*

Quiz 35
Question 10

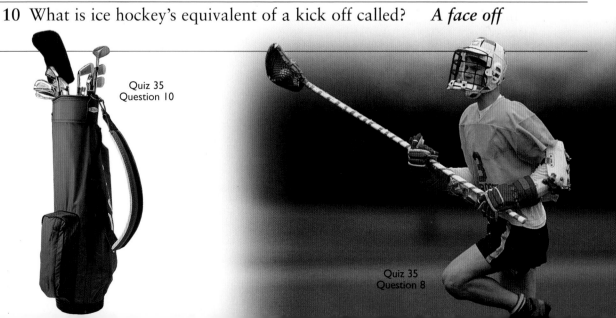

Quiz 35
Question 8

Quiz 35
Terminology Teasers

Questions	Answers
1 In which sport is a Boston crab a painful experience for the recipient?	*Wrestling*
2 What name is given to the frame with metal spikes that is strapped to a mountaineer's boot?	*A crampon*
3 In cricket, what are cover point and short leg?	*Fielding positions*
4 In which sport is Oklahoma the name of a defensive formation?	*American football*
5 What are the long, baggy knee length knickerbockers usually associated with golf known as?	*Plus Fours*
6 What name is given to a boxer who leads with his right hand?	*Southpaw*
7 On a yacht, what is a burgee?	*An ornamental flag*
8 In which sport is a stick called a crosse used?	*Lacrosse*
9 What is known as the Sport of Kings?	*Horse racing*
10 In which sport is a mulligan a free stroke?	*Golf*

Quiz 36
Question 7

Quiz 36
Question 2

Quiz 38

For the Little Leaguers

Questions	Answers
1 What are rugby players doing if they are selling dummies?	*Pretending to pass the ball*
2 In which Japanese sport do wrestlers attempt to push each other out of a ring?	*Sumo wrestling*
3 Which of the following sports do horses not take part in: polo, dressage or hurling?	*Hurling*
4 Which member of England's 2002 World Cup squad has the first name of Solberg?	*Sol Campbell*
5 How many runs have been scored in a maiden over in cricket?	*None*
6 What name is given to the small peg from which a golf ball is driven?	*The tee*
7 What is the official national sport of the United States?	*Baseball*
8 In which sport do competitors perform a Fosbury Flop?	*High jump*
9 Are the home shirts of Italy's national soccer team red, blue or yellow?	*Blue*
10 In which sport do participants say *touché* if a hit has been scored?	*Fencing*

Quiz 37
Question 3

Quiz 37
Question 6

Quiz 37

Questions	Answers
1 What name is given to the area surrounding the golf hole where a putter is used?	*The green*
2 What game is played using the fruit of the horse chestnut tree?	*Conkers*
3 Which of the following sports uses a mallet: billiards, croquet or hockey?	*Croquet*
4 Which British city hosted the Commonwealth Games in 2002?	*Manchester*
5 In tenpin bowling, what is a strike?	*Knocking down all the pins with one ball*
6 Which member of England's 2006 World Cup squad has sons called Brooklyn, Romeo and Cruz?	*David Beckham*
7 Who would deliver a Yorker: a javelin thrower, a boxer or a cricket bowler?	*A cricket bowler*
8 Which ball is worth seven points in snooker?	*The black ball*
9 What is the American football equivalent of a try in rugby?	*A touchdown*
10 How many serves is a tennis player allowed per point?	*Two*

Quiz 38
Question 4

Quiz 40
A Sports Bag

Questions	Answers

Questions

1 Which is the only country to have played in every World Cup finals from 1930 to 2006?

2 In 1986, who became World Heavyweight Boxing Champion after defeating Trevor Berbick?

3 In which city did Australian rules football originate?

4 In gymnastics, what is a backwards handspring known as?

5 What sport is played by the Doncaster Belles?
Quiz 39 Question 4

6 Is the Happy Valley horse racing course in New York, Paris or Hong Kong?

7 What piece of sporting equipment shares its name with a character from *A Midsummer Nights Dream*?

8 In what type of car did Paddy Hopkirk and Henry Widden win the 1964 Monte Carlo Rally?

9 In archery, what is a bluffie?

10 In which month is the Epsom Derby traditionally held?

Answers

Brazil

Mike Tyson

Melbourne

A flic flac

Soccer

Hong Kong

Puck

A Mini

A practice shot

June

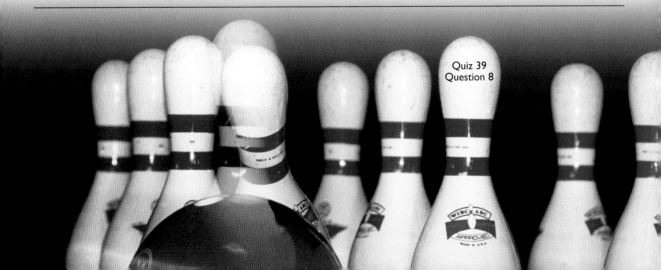

Quiz 39
Question 8

Quiz 39
A Sports Bag

Questions	Answers
1 In which country did speed skating originate?	*The Netherlands*
2 Who recorded his first of nine Epsom Derby wins on a horse called Never Say Die?	*Lester Piggott*
3 Which British athlete broke the world record for the javelin in 1990?	*Steve Backley*
4 Which sporting body has the initials WBO?	*World Boxing Organisation*
5 In which country was the 1990 soccer World Cup held: Italy, Spain or France?	*Italy*
6 Bernard Hinault is a national hero in France for his endeavours in which sport?	*Cycling*
7 Where does Old Father Time appear at Lord's Cricket Ground?	*On the weather vane*
8 In which sport might you achieve a strike or a spare?	*Tenpin bowling*
9 Who became Formula One World Champion after winning the Japanese Grand Prix in October 1996?	*Damon Hill*
10 Ice Dance champions Torvill and Dean are most associated with which piece of music?	*Ravel's* Bolero

Quiz 40
Question 7

Quiz 40
Question 8

Basketball Bonanza

Questions	Answers
1 What is the name of Utah's basketball team, is it Utah Rocks, Utah Motown or Utah Jazz?	*Utah Jazz*
2 What is a basketball coach indicating when forming a letter T with the hands?	*Time out*
3 Which legendary basketball star amassed a career total of 29,277 points for the Chicago Bulls?	*Michael Jordan*
4 Which nation did the United States beat in the final of the men's basketball at the Sydney Olympics?	*France*
5 In which decade was the first NBA Championships contested in the United States: 1930s, 1940s or 1950s?	*1940s*
6 From which country do the Vancouver Grizzlies hail?	*Canada*
7 How many players are in a basketball team?	*Five*
8 Which Greek team won the Euroleague Basketball Championships in 2002?	*Panathinaikos*
9 Which nation beat the United States in the 1972 Olympic final with a score of 51-50?	*The U.S.S.R.*
10 What is the name of the basketball team in the English town of Reading: the Rockets or the Raiders ?	*Rockets*

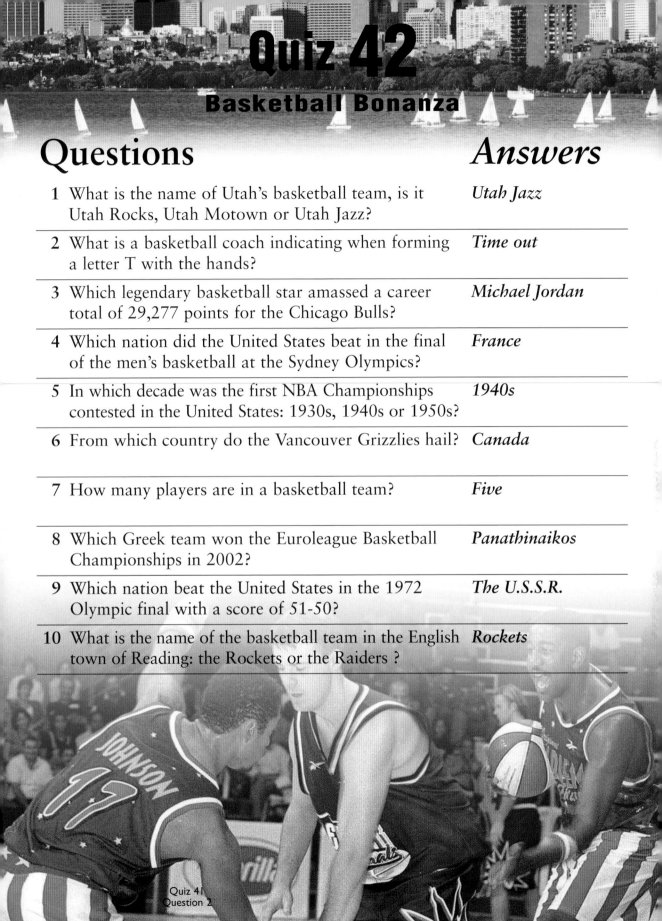

Quiz 41
Question 2

Quiz 41
Basketball Bonanza

Questions	Answers
1 Which of the following is the name of a basketball team in Detroit: the Engines, Pistons or Wheelers?	*Pistons*
2 Which touring basketball team was captained for many years by Meadowlark Lemon?	*Harlem Globetrotters*
3 Which U.S. basketball team changed their name from the Bullets to the Wizards?	*Washington Wizards*
4 In an NBA basketball game, how many minutes are played in each quarter?	*12 minutes*
5 What do the initials WBL stand for?	*World Basketball League*
6 In which state do the Boston Celtics play their home matches?	*Massachusetts*
7 How many teams contested the NBA Championship in its inaugural year: 11, 12 or 13?	*11*
8 What is the basketball equivalent of a kick off called?	*A tip off*
9 In 1998, Kinder Bologna were the European League Basketball Champions. What is their home country?	*Italy*
10 What is the name of the basketball team in the English city of Coventry: The Crusaders, Cavaliers or Cruisers?	*The Crusaders*

Quiz 42
Question 3

Quiz 44
A Sports Bag

Questions	Answers
	Quiz 43 Question 7
1 What nationality is former Wimbledon winner Bjorn Borg?	*Swedish*
2 What article of clothing is presented to the winner of golf's U.S. Masters?	*A green jacket*
3 Which European country won the men's World Hockey Championship for the third time in 1998?	*The Netherlands*
4 For which club did Alan Shearer score his first Football League goal?	*Southampton*
5 Which duo did Betty Calloway coach to a Winter Olympic gold medal?	*Torvill and Dean*
6 In which card game would a competitor score a grand slam whilst attempting to win the Bermuda Bowl?	*Bridge*
7 Which country did Richard Hadlee represent at cricket?	*New Zealand*
8 Which British athlete won the gold medal for the 100 m at the 1992 Olympics?	*Linford Christie*
9 Which Scottish golf course has a hole called the Postage Stamp?	*Troon*
10 Who was appointed manager of the England soccer team in 1996?	*Glenn Hoddle*

Quiz 43
Question 8

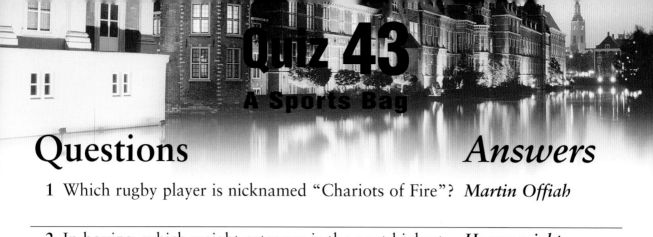

Quiz 43
A Sports Bag

Questions	Answers
1 Which rugby player is nicknamed "Chariots of Fire"?	*Martin Offiah*
2 In boxing, which weight category is the next highest after cruiserweight?	*Heavyweight*
3 What first was achieved by Alex Greaves in the Epsom Derby?	*First woman to ride in the Derby*
4 What is the meteorological nickname of the snooker star Alex Higgins?	*"Hurricane"*
5 From which club did Manchester United sign Eric Cantona?	*Leeds United*
6 Eddie Merckx is a legendary name in which sport?	*Cycling*
7 Which ball in snooker is worth six points?	*The pink ball*
8 In which sport did Michelle Smith win Olympic medals?	*Swimming*
9 What nationality is the jockey Pat Eddery?	*Irish*
10 What is the name of the home ground of Real Madrid soccer club?	*Bernabeu Stadium*

Quiz 44
Question 5

Quiz 46
A Sports Bag

Questions	Answers
1 Leighton Rees, the first ever darts World Champion, was born in which country?	*Wales*
2 What is the name of the machine that picks up the pins in tenpin bowling?	*Pin spotter*
3 How many players comprise a beach volleyball team?	*Two*
4 Which 1966 World Cup winner went on to manage the Republic of Ireland in the World Cup finals?	*Jack Charlton*
5 In the United States, in which sport is the Royal Rumble contested?	*Wrestling*
6 In which sport is a series of bouts called a barrage?	*Fencing*
7 Who inflicted a defeat on Mike Tyson in November 1996?	*Evander Holyfield*
8 Three cushions is a form of which indoor game?	*Billiards*
9 In which country did Gary Lineker play for Grampus 8?	*Japan*
10 What is the age limit for racehorses in nursery stakes?	*Two year olds*

Quiz 45
Question 9

Quiz 45

A Sports Bag

Questions	Answers
1 At the soccer World Cup of 1998, which nation were known as "The Reggae Boys"?	*Jamaica*
2 Where did the 2002 Winter Olympics take place?	*Salt Lake City, U.S.A.*
3 Which monocle-wearing boxer made his ring entrances to Tina Turner's hit *Simply The Best*?	*Chris Eubank*
4 Which Italian Chelsea star scored the quickest ever goal in the FA Cup final in 1997?	*Robert Di Matteo*
5 Which sport takes place in a velodrome?	*Cycling*
6 At which sport was Kate Howey of Great Britain a World Champion in 1998?	*Judo*
7 Who did Mary Decker collide with in the 1984 Olympic 3000 m final?	*Zola Budd*
8 What six-letter word is the name given to the member of a rowing team who sets the rowing pace?	*The stroke*
9 Which English cricketer scored his 100th century in 1895?	*W. G. Grace*
10 Who connects the New York Yankees and Marilyn Monroe?	*Joe DiMaggio*

Quiz 46
Question 6

Quiz 46
Question 5

Questions	Answers
1 Which Wimbledon champion was called up for military service in 2001?	*Goran Ivanisevic*
2 Which Swedish tennis star won the men's singles at the 1988 U.S. Open?	*Mats Wilander*
3 Which of the four Grand Slam tournaments is played in the southern hemisphere?	*The Australian Open*
4 In 1989, who won the men's singles at the French Open when he was just 17 years of age?	*Michael Chang*
5 Which British tennis star was married to Chris Evert?	*John Lloyd*
6 What nationality is the tennis star Thomas Muster?	*Austrian*
7 Who won his fifth Wimbledon title in 1998?	*Pete Sampras*
8 Which female tennis star wrote a novel called *Total Zone*?	*Martina Navratilova*
9 How did Guenter Parche make news headlines in Hamburg in 1993?	*He stabbed Monica Seles on court*
10 Who lifted the women's singles title at Wimbledon in 2001?	*Venus Williams*

Quiz 47
Question 8

Quiz 47

Anyone For Tennis?

Questions	Answers
1 Which fellow German beat Boris Becker in the 1991 Wimbledon final?	*Michael Stich*
2 What was Evonne Cawley called when she won her first Wimbledon singles title?	*Evonne Goolagong*
3 Which tennis star of yesteryear was nicknamed "Little Mo"?	*Maureen Connelly*
4 Where is the International Tennis Hall of Fame located?	*Newport, Rhode Island, U.S.A.*
5 What nationality is Ilie Nastase?	*Romanian*
6 Which Australian tennis star of the 1960s was nicknamed "The Rockhampton Rocket"?	*Rod Laver*
7 In which city is the U.S. Open contested?	*New York*
8 Who acquired the nickname of "Super Brat" after shouting out "You cannot be serious" at Wimbledon?	*John McEnroe*
9 What is the minimum number of points that must be won in a game for the score to reach deuce?	*Six*
10 Was Andre Agassi born in Chicago, Las Vegas or Seattle?	*Las Vegas*

Quiz 48
Question 10

A Sports Bag of Anagrams

Unravel the following anagrams
in the given subjects

Answers

1	EAR KAT	A sport	*Karate*
2	CAR LOSES	A sport	*Lacrosse*
3	VETS CREAM	A male sports star	*Steve Cram*
4	FLICK A DON	A male sports star	*Nick Faldo*
5	ODD BAR RAT	Sporting equipment	*Dartboard*
6	PATCH TWOS	Sporting equipment	*Stopwatch*
7	NO LAVA LIST	Soccer team	*Aston Villa*
8	NAIL CAVE	Soccer team	*Valencia*
9	NOSE IS CAMEL	Female sports star	*Monica Seles*
10	LOOK AT GRUB	Female sports star	*Olga Korbut*

Quiz 49
Question 4

A Sports Bag of Anagrams

Unravel the following anagrams
in the given subjects

Answers

	Anagram	Subject	Answer
1	FLOG	A sport	*Golf*
2	BARD IS ILL	A sport	*Billiards*
3	MAN HIT MEN	A male sports star	*Tim Henman*
4	I NO CHEW MEAL	A male sports star	*Michael Owen*
5	POOL STAGS	Sporting equipment	*Goalposts*
6	WE STICK	Sporting equipment	*Wickets*
7	DREAM LAIRD	Soccer team	*Real Madrid*
8	BEAR NEED	Soccer team	*Aberdeen*
9	IM TRAINING ASH	Female sports star	*Martina Hingis*
10	SHINE FAR SOIL	Female sports star	*Alison Fisher*

Quiz 50
Question 6

Quiz 50
Question 4

Questions	Answers
1 In which sport is the Preakness Stakes contested in Baltimore?	Horse racing
2 What is the shortest distance over which swimming races are held in the Olympic games?	50 m
3 In the game of golf what is measured by a stimpmeter?	The pace of the green
4 In which sport did Audley Harrison win an Olympic gold medal?	Boxing
5 Which country hosted soccer's World Cup in 1970 and 1986?	Mexico
6 Who did Peter Ebdon beat in the final of the 2002 Snooker World Championship?	Stephen Hendry
7 What seed was Boris Becker when he won his first Wimbledon title?	He was unseeded
8 Does the judo term *dan* mean: expert, leader or belt?	Leader
9 Which city won the vote to host the 2012 Olympic Games?	London
10 20, 1, 18, which number comes next in a dartboard sequence?	Four

Quiz 52
Question 1

Quiz 52
Question 8

20

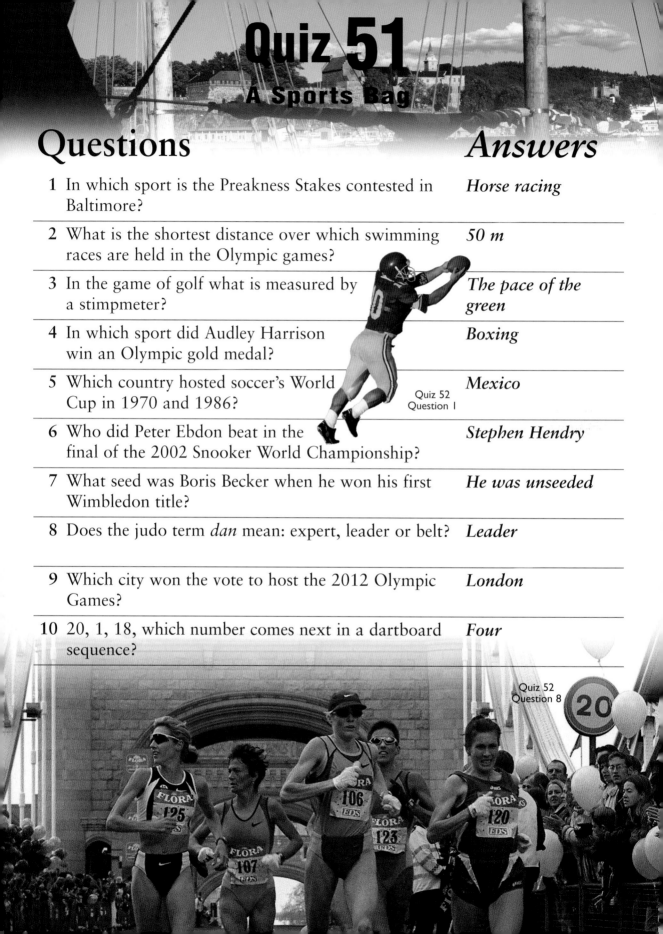

Quiz 52

A Sports Bag

Questions	Answers
1 Which sport featured in the Denzel Washington film *Remember The Titans?*	*American football*
2 What was the name of the suffragette who threw herself under the king's horse in the 1913 Derby?	*Emily Davidson*
3 Which London soccer club has a cannon on its badge?	*Arsenal*
4 In the game of cricket what has a maximum width of 10.8 cm?	*Cricket bat*
5 Which was the first country in Asia to host the Winter Olympics?	*Japan*
6 Which war did Muhammed Ali refuse to fight in resulting in the removal of his world title?	*The Vietnam War*
7 In which sport are the Eisenhower Trophy and the Curtis Cup contested?	*Golf*
8 Which annual sporting event has been sponsored by Guinness, Mars, ADT and Flora?	*The London Marathon*
9 In which European capital city is the Bislett Stadium?	*Oslo*
10 Which French striker was sent off in a 2002 World Cup match against Uruguay?	*Thierry Henry*

Quiz 51
Question 5

Quiz 51
Question 4

Questions	Answers
1 Father of Michael and Jeff, Uncle of Jolen: who is this famous racing driver?	*Mario Andretti*
2 Which Grand Prix racing team are based in Woking, in the county of Surrey?	*McClaren*
3 Over how many laps is The Indianapolis 500 contested?	*200*
4 Which Blackburn born motorcyclist clinched his first World Superbikes titles in 1994?	*Carl Fogarty*
5 In which country is the Suzuka motor racing circuit?	*Japan*
6 Which car company manufactured Chris Boardman's gold medal winning bicycle at the Barcelona Olympics?	*Lotus*
7 Which 1990 film, starring Tom Cruise, was set against the NASCAR racing circuit?	Days of Thunder
8 What is the name for the heavily customized cars, popular in the United States?	*Hot rods*
9 At which motor racing circuit was Ayrton Senna killed?	*Imola*
10 Who is the billionaire owner of Formula One?	*Bernie Ecclestone*

Quiz 53
Question 9

Quiz 53
Motor Sport Mania

Questions	Answers
1 Who was the first British driver to be Formula One World Champion?	*Mike Hawthorn*
2 In which month is the Indianapolis 500 traditionally staged?	*May*
3 Who won the Isle of Man TT senior race in June 2002?	*Dave Jeffries*
4 In which country was the driver Niki Lauda born?	*Austria*
5 Which race, first held in May 1923, was won by Andre Lagache and Rene Leonard?	*Le Mans*
6 What name is given to the front position at the start of a motor race?	*Pole position*
7 In which country is the motor racing circuit of Estoril?	*Portugal*
8 In 1959, which British car became the first to win the World Sports Car Championships?	*Aston Martin*
9 In 1995, which Scottish driver became the youngest ever World Champion in rally driving?	*Colin McRae*
10 Who was the only driver to win the Formula One World Championship posthumously?	*Jochen Rindt*

Quiz 54
Question 8

Quiz 56
A Sports Bag

Questions	Answers
1 In which city did Lennox Lewis beat Mike Tyson in June 2002?	*Memphis*
2 Which West Indian fast bowler died in 1999 aged 41?	*Malcolm Marshall*
3 What three-letter word is the name given to a replayed point in tennis?	*Let*
4 In which sport did Dawn Fraser compete in three consecutive Olympics?	*Swimming*
5 In which weight category did the Irish boxer Barry McGuigan become World Champion?	*Featherweight*
6 The Duckworth Lewis method is used to keep the score in which sport?	*Cricket*
7 Katarina Witt became a leading exponent in which sport?	*Ice-skating*
8 In which country do the soccer team Twente Enschede play their home matches?	*Netherlands*
9 Did the game of polo originate in India, Persia or Argentina?	*Persia (Iran)*
10 Which military activist is tattooed on Mike Tyson's torso?	*Che Guevara*

Quiz 55
Question 5

Quiz 55
Question 1

Quiz 55
A Sports Bag

Questions	Answers
1 In which court game must players wear special lensed eyewear and wrist thongs in the warm-up?	*Racketball*
2 Which country played its first ever cricket test match in 1982?	*Sri Lanka*
3 Which medal did Fatima Whitbread win in the 1988 Olympics: gold, silver or bronze?	*Silver*
4 In 1990, which country became the first African nation to reach the quarter final in soccer's World Cup?	*Cameroon*
5 Which animal do you associate with Chicago's American football team?	*A bear*
6 What is the surname of the Australian cricketing brothers Trevor, Ian and Greg?	*Chappell*
7 In which country do the soccer team Osasuna play their home matches?	*Spain*
8 Who was the last British player to win a Wimbledon singles title in the 20th century?	*Virginia Wade*
9 Who succeeded Bill Shankly as the manager of Liverpool?	*Bob Paisley*
10 What was won in June 2002 by High Chaparral?	*The Epsom Derby*

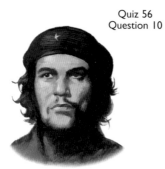

Quiz 56
Question 10

Quiz 56
Question 7

Quiz 58
Sporting Heroes

Questions	Answers
1 Who scored England's penalty when beating Argentina 1-0 in the 2002 World Cup?	*David Beckham*
2 In 1954, who set an historical landmark in athletics, with a time of 3 minutes 59.4 seconds?	*Roger Bannister*
3 When world rankings were first introduced into tennis, who was the first man to be ranked No. 1?	*Ilie Nastase*
4 Who ran the fastest 100 m in the 20th century?	*Maurice Greene*
5 Who won six world snooker titles in the 1980s?	*Steve Davis*
6 Who was named Female Athlete of the Century by the International Athletics Federation?	*Fanny Blankers-Koen*
7 Who was the first footballer to win 100 caps for England?	*Billy Wright*
8 In 1952, who retired as undefeated World Heavyweight Boxing Champion?	*Rocky Marciano*
9 Which female tennis star won the French Open and the Australian Open in 2001?	*Jennifer Capriati*
10 Who was the first jockey to receive a knighthood?	*Sir Gordon Richards*

Quiz 57
Question 2

Quiz 57

Sporting Heroes

Questions	Answers
1 In which sport did Matthew Pinsent win an Olympic gold medal in 2000?	*Rowing*
2 Which Portuguese soccer star was voted European Footballer of the Year in 2000?	*Luis Figo*
3 What is the real first name of the basketball superstar Michael Jordan?	*Earvin*
4 Damon Hill won the Formula One World Championship driving for which racing team?	*Williams-Renault*
5 Who was the first man to run 1500 m in under 3 minutes 30 seconds?	*Said Aouita*
6 Which boxer of yesteryear was nicknamed "the Manassa Mauler"?	*Jack Dempsey*
7 Who scored England's second goal in the 1966 World Cup final?	*Martin Peters*
8 What does the T stand for in the name of Ian T. Botham: Terence, Thomas or Tarquin?	*Terence*
9 Who ran the fastest 200 m of the 20th century?	*Michael Johnson*
10 Who is the youngest footballer to have scored for England in the 20th century?	*Michael Owen*

Quiz 58
Question 4

Quiz 60

Formula One Facts

Questions	Answers
1 Who was the only South African driver to be crowned Formula One World Champion in the 20th century?	*Jodie Schekter*
2 What nationality is Mika Hakkinen?	*Finnish*
3 In which country is the Monza Grand Prix circuit?	*Italy*
4 Which leading name in Formula One won his first Grand Prix in 1985, in Portugal?	*Ayrton Senna*
5 Who was ordered to pull over in the 2002 Austrian Grand Prix to allow Michael Schumacher to win?	*Rubens Barrichello*
6 Who was the first driver to win a Formula One Grand Prix in a car he made himself?	*Jack Brabham*
7 Which British course staged the first ever Formula One World Championship race?	*Silverstone*
8 Which driver was the BBC Sports Personality of the Year in 1992?	*Nigel Mansell*
9 Which was the first communist country to stage a Formula One Grand Prix?	*Hungary*
10 Which car manufacturer was the first to win 100 Formula One Grand Prix races?	*Ferrari*

Quiz 59
Question 4

Questions	Answers
1 Who was the first North American driver to be crowned Formula One World Champion?	*Phil Hill*
2 What is the name of Michael Schumacher's racing brother?	*Ralf*
3 Which British driver finished runner up in the 1999 Formula One World Championships?	*Eddie Irvine*
4 Which Argentinean driver was the first man to win five Formula One world titles?	*Juan Manuel Fangio*
5 In which country is the Sepang Grand Prix circuit?	*Malaysia*
6 Who was the first Formula One driver to register 50 Grand Prix wins?	*Alain Prost*
7 What was the name of Damon Hill's father, who was also a Formula One World Champion?	*Graham Hill*
8 In which city is the Hungarian Grand Prix contested?	*Budapest*
9 For which racing team did Jensen Button drive in the 2002 Formula One World Championships?	*Renault*
10 Who was the first Brazilian driver to be crowned Formula One World Champion?	*Emerson Fittipaldi*

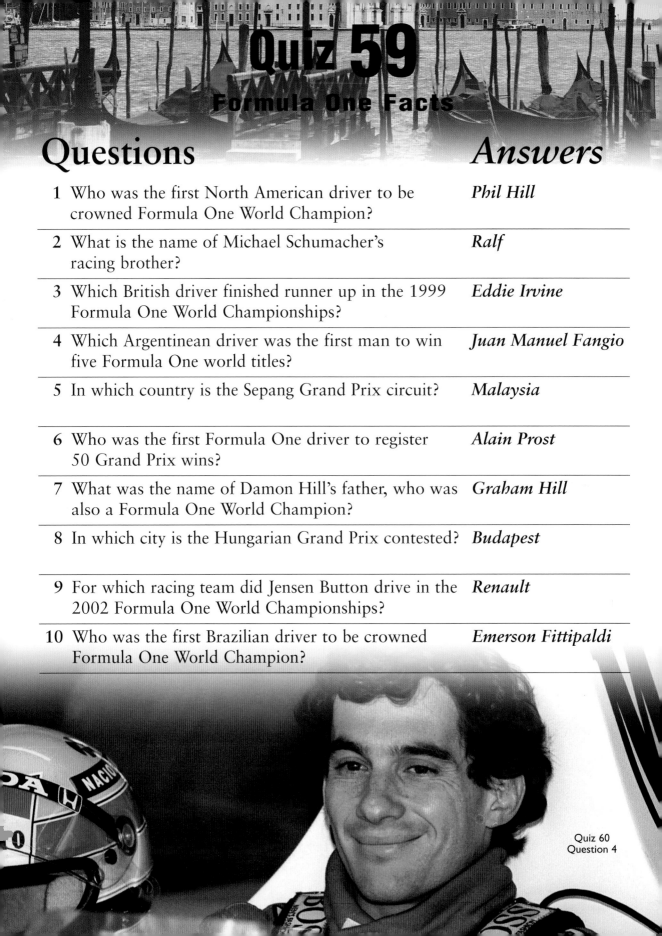

Quiz 60
Question 4

Quiz 62
A Sports Bag

Questions	Answers
1 What connects the Summer Olympic venues of 1904, 1932, 1984 and 1996?	*All were venues in the United States*
2 Who was disqualified from the 1995 Wimbledon men's singles for hitting a ball against a ball girl?	*Tim Henman*
3 What caused Rome to withdraw its application to host the 1908 Summer Olympics?	*A volcanic eruption*
4 In which sport was a Lonsdale Belt first awarded in 1909?	*Boxing*
5 In which city do Hearts face Hibs in a derby match?	*Edinburgh*
6 What do the initials FDC mean to a stamp collector?	*First day cover*
7 Which was the only European country to host the Winter Olympics three times in the 20th century?	*France*
8 Which goalkeeper played his 1000th Football League game, whilst playing for Leyton Orient?	*Peter Shilton*
9 Which U.S. tennis player won the women's singles gold medal for tennis at the 1996 Olympics?	*Lindsay Davenport*
10 Who did Liverpool beat in the final of the 2001 UEFA Cup?	*Alaves*

Quiz 61
Question 7

Quiz 61
A Sports Bag

Questions	Answers
1 Which Italian opera singer sang at the 2000 Sydney Olympics?	*Andrea Bocelli*
2 What was stolen in March 1966 that made news headlines?	*The World Cup*
3 Which German club did Nottingham Forest beat in the final of the 1980 European Cup?	*SV Hamburg*
4 Which country were cricket World Champions in 1983?	*India*
5 The King George V Cup is contested at Hickstead in which sport?	*Show jumping*
6 Which horse racing trainer penned the 2005 autobiography *My Colourful Life from Red to Amber*?	*Ginger McCain*
7 Ted Hankey, Phil Taylor and Dennis Priestly have all been World Champions at what sport?	*Darts*
8 How many points are awarded to a driver who finishes first in a Formula One Grand Prix race?	*Ten points*
9 Who was the last female European winner of the Wimbledon singles in the 20th century?	*Jana Novotna*
10 Which club did Manchester United beat with a last minute goal in the final of the 1999 European Cup?	*Bayern Munich*

Quiz 62
Question 3

Quiz 64

For the Little Leaguers

Questions	Answers
1 Which bird provides the nickname of Sheffield Wednesday F.C.?	*An owl*
2 Paul Gascoigne played for which club in the Scottish Premier League?	*Rangers*
3 Which animal takes part in point to point races and steeplechases?	*The horse*
4 What is the surname of the tennis playing sisters Venus and Serena?	*Williams*
5 For which country did Raul play in the 2002 World Cup?	*Spain*
6 What shape of ball would you associate with Jona Lomu?	*Oval (Rugby)*
7 How many wheels does a unicycle have?	*One*
8 Which soccer team is sometimes referred to by the initials WBA?	*West Bromwich Albion*
9 What first name is shared by the footballers Maradona and Forlan?	*Diego*
10 In which sport are the Golden Gloves Championships contested?	*Boxing*

Quiz 63
Question 9

Quiz 63
For the Little Leaguers

Questions	Answers
1 Where on the body are flippers worn?	*The feet*
2 In tennis, what V word means hitting the ball before it bounces?	*Volley*
3 How many points have been scored in a maximum break in snooker?	*147*
4 In darts what is the highest score that can be made with one dart?	*60 (Treble 20)*
5 Which country did Dieter Hamman play for in the 2002 World Cup?	*Germany*
6 How many bishops are on a chessboard at the start of a game?	*Four*
7 In which TV show are Ally McCoist and Frankie Dettori opposing team captains?	**A Question of Sport**
8 Which soccer club is sometimes referred to by the initials QPR?	*Queens Park Rangers*
9 Which marine creature forms part of the name of Miami's American football team?	*Dolphin*
10 What last name is shared by the soccer teams Tranmere and Blackburn?	*Rovers*

Quiz 64
Question 7

Quiz 64
Question 3

Quiz 64
Question 1

Quiz 66

It's a Goal!!

Questions	Answers
1 In which sport is a chukka a period of play?	Polo
2 Which city do the Maple Leafs ice hockey team come from?	Toronto
3 Which Italian striker was the leading scorer at the 1982 World Cup finals?	Paulo Rossi
4 In which sport are Dublin, Down and Kerry all past winners of the All Ireland Championships?	Gaelic football
5 Who did England play in their first international rugby union match?	Scotland
6 Who did a striker named Pauleta, score a hat trick for against Poland in the 2002 World Cup?	Portugal
7 Which team appeared in four consecutive Super Bowls from 1991 to 1994?	Buffalo Bills
8 In which sport is the Camanachd Association Challenge Cup contested?	Shinty
9 In Australian rules football is the substitute known as the 18th man or the 19th man?	19th man
10 In ice hockey, what name is given to the central area between the defence and the attack zones?	The neutral zone

Quiz 65
Question 6

Quiz 65

It's a Goal!!

Questions	Answers
1 How many players make up a hurling team?	*15*
2 At which sport do the Brisbane Lions play the Adelaide Crows?	*Australian rules football*
3 How many goals did France score in total in the 2002 World Cup?	*Zero*
4 In Australian rules football how many points are awarded for a goal?	*Six*
5 In American football, which team won the Super Bowl in 2002?	*New England Patriots*
6 Which TV presenter scored 48 goals for the England soccer team?	*Gary Lineker*
7 In which sport has Sean Kerly captained England?	*Hockey*
8 Lacrosse is the official national sport of which country?	*Canada*
9 Is a polo pony allowed to score a goal by kicking the ball through the posts?	*Yes*
10 In ice hockey, which member of the team has the letter A on the uniform?	*Assistant team captain*

Quiz 66
Question 1

Quiz 66
Question 2

Quiz 68
A Sports Bag

Questions	Answers
1 How many players comprise a handball team?	*Seven*
2 What is Frankie short for in the name of the jockey Frankie Dettori?	*Lanfranco*
3 Which Sunderland goalkeeper kept goal for Denmark in the 2002 soccer World Cup?	*Thomas Sorensen*
4 What type of sporting contest includes calf roping and bull riding events?	*Rodeo*
5 At which English course is the 1000 Guineas horse race run?	*Newmarket*
6 When a batsman scores a duck in both innings what phrase is used?	*A pair of spectacles*
7 Which Italian soccer club did Sven Goran Eriksson leave to manage England?	*Lazio*
8 In which sport do competitors make the Liffey Descent?	*Canoeing*
9 Mills Lane is a leading referee in which sport?	*Boxing*
10 Which sports company took their name from an African gazelle?	*Reebok*

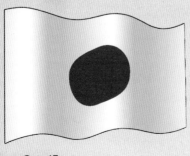

Quiz 67
Question 6

Quiz 67
A Sports Bag

Questions	Answers
1 Who were England playing in the 1990 soccer World Cup when Paul Gascoigne broke down in tears?	*Germany*
2 Which game is played at the Yankee Stadium?	*Baseball*
3 What is the name of the village in Berkshire where Queen Anne established a famous horseracing course?	*Ascot*
4 In 1981, Sue Brown was the first woman to compete in which sporting event?	*The Oxford and Cambridge Boat Race*
5 Name the Newcastle United keeper who kept goal for the Republic of Ireland in the 2002 World Cup.	*Shay Given*
6 In which country did karate originate?	*Japan*
7 What does the word Olympiad mean?	*Every four years*
8 What name is given to the skiing event where competitors have to swerve in and out to avoid flags?	*Slalom*
9 Who did Alex Ferguson succeed as manager of Manchester United?	*Ron Atkinson*
10 What do the initials PU signify in the form guide of a racehorse?	*Pulled up*

Quiz 68
Question 6

Quiz 68
Question 4

Questions	Answers
1 Which Welshman did Steve Davis beat in the final when winning his first world snooker title?	*Doug Mountjoy*
2 What was the second German city to host the Summer Olympics?	*Munich*
3 Which British female hurdler set a new world record at the 1993 World Athletics Championships?	*Sally Gunnell*
4 At which sporting venue can spectators view races from the Paddock Hill Grandstand?	*Brands Hatch*
5 Which Grand Slam tennis tournament was won by Bjorn Borg on six separate occasions?	*The French Open*
6 Which former England cricketer shares his name with a small breed of dog?	*Jack Russell*
7 What sport is played by the Nottingham Panthers?	*Ice hockey*
8 What type of flower features on the badge of Glamorgan's county cricket club?	*The daffodil*
9 Who married Tatum O'Neal in 1986?	*John McEnroe*
10 In the United States, what ended in March 1995 after lasting for 232 days?	*The baseball players' strike*

Quiz 69
Question 7

Quiz 69
Question 5

Quiz **69**

A Sports Bag

Questions	Answers
1 At which sports venue do horses gallop around Tattenham Corner?	*Epsom*
2 Which European capital city was the first city to host the modern Olympics on two occasions?	*Paris*
3 In which U.S. state is the Augusta Golf Course?	*Georgia*
4 How many lions are on the shirts of England's soccer team?	*Three*
5 What type of fruit stands on top of the men's singles tennis trophy for Wimbledon?	*A pineapple*
6 In which country were the Commonwealth Games first held?	*Canada*
7 At the Seoul Olympics, which tennis star won Argentina's first gold medal for 16 years?	*Gabriella Sabatini*
8 The snatch and the clean and jerk are the two standard lifts in which sport?	*Weightlifting*
9 Dennis Lillee took 355 test wickets for which country?	*Australia*
10 What word describes the last movement of an exercise when a gymnast descends from the apparatus?	*Dismount*

Quiz 70
Question 6

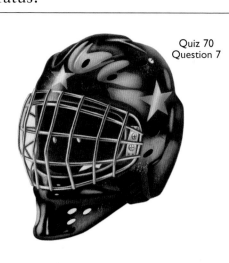

Quiz 70
Question 7

Quiz 72

Soccer Crazy

Questions	Answers
1 Which Spanish club has been managed by Bobby Robson and Terry Venables?	*Barcelona*
2 In which European country is the headquarters of FIFA?	*Switzerland*
3 Who was the first British king to attend an FA Cup final?	*George V (in 1914)*
4 Which Irish club play their home matches at Windsor Park?	*Linfield*
5 In 1996, who became the first foreign footballer to captain an FA Cup winning side?	*Eric Cantona*
6 Who was the first footballer to be voted European Footballer of the Year on three separate occasions?	*Johan Cruyff*
7 Which Scottish soccer club are nicknamed "The Bhoys"?	*Celtic*
8 What was the score in the 1970 World Cup final?	*Brazil 4 Italy 1*
9 CRY YET BOUND is an anagram of which soccer club?	*Derby County*
10 Which country's international team are nicknamed "The Pharaohs"?	*Egypt*

Quiz 71
Question 1

Quiz 71
Question 4

Quiz 71
Soccer Crazy

Questions	Answers
1 Which South American country do Boca Juniors come from?	*Argentina*
2 Who managed England's soccer team during Euro 2000?	*Kevin Keegan*
3 What is the oldest Scottish League club?	*Queen's Park*
4 Who became the first British footballer to be transferred for £15 million?	*Alan Shearer*
5 Which is the only British league club with the last name Academicals?	*Hamilton*
6 Which part of a pig's body provides the nickname of Bolton Wanderers?	*"Trotters"*
7 Who scored for both sides in the 1987 FA Cup final when Coventry beat Tottenham?	*Gary Mabbutt*
8 STICKY TOE is an anagram of which soccer club?	*Stoke City*
9 In January 2002, who set a new Premiership record by scoring in eight consecutive games?	*Ruud van Nistelrooy*
10 The Bobby Moore Stand can be found at which soccer club's ground?	*West Ham United*

Quiz 72
Question 2

Quiz 72
Question 3

Quiz 74
A Sports Bag

Questions	Answers
1 A bronze statue of which horse was unveiled at Aintree in 1988?	*Red Rum*
2 Who came last in the 1988 Winter Olympic ski jump competition for men?	*Eddie "The Eagle" Edwards*
3 Do the Harvard Rules govern baseball or American football?	*American football*
4 In which ball sport is the ball hit onto the service penthouse?	*Real tennis*
5 Which chess term describes the situation when neither player can win the game?	*Stalemate*
6 Which sport do we associate with Glorious Goodwood?	*Horse racing*
7 Which snooker manager and boxing promoter took over at Leyton Orient F.C. in 1995?	*Barry Hearn*
8 What is the official language of the Olympic games?	*French*
9 Which sport is played by the Wigan Warriors?	*Rugby league*
10 At which sport did Fred Perry become World Champion in 1929?	*Table tennis*

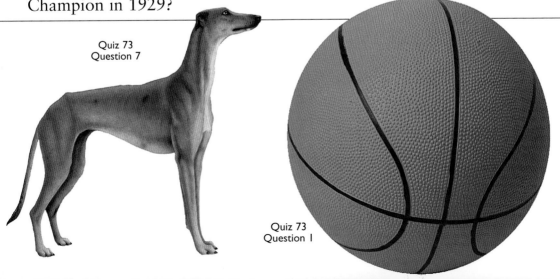

Quiz 73
Question 7

Quiz 73
Question 1

Quiz 73
A Sports Bag

Questions	Answers
1 In which sport does play commence with a tip off?	*Basketball*
2 What is the alternative name for the hop, step and jump?	*The triple jump*
3 How old must a horse be to take part in a steeplechase race?	*Four years old*
4 Who declared the 1936 Olympics officially open?	*Adolf Hitler*
5 Which is the older in golf, the British Open or the U.S. Open?	*The British Open*
6 What is the name of the bars on which female gymnasts compete?	*The asymmetric bars*
7 Which sport is governed by a body with the initials GRA?	*Greyhound racing*
8 At the start of a game of draughts how many pieces does each player have?	*12*
9 At which stadium did Manchester United win the European Cup in 1999?	*Nou Camp in Barcelona*
10 Which was the first European country to host soccer's World Cup?	*Italy in 1934*

Quiz 74
Question 3

Questions | Answers

	Questions	Answers
1	At which Canadian venue did Daley Thompson compete in his first Olympics in 1976?	*Montreal*
2	Which U.S. tennis player was Wimbledon men's singles champion in 1974 and 1982?	*Jimmy Connors*
3	In golf, who won the U.S. Masters in 1997 at the age of 21?	*Tiger Woods*
4	Who scored in the 1958 soccer World Cup final aged just 17?	*Pele*
5	Who was the first ever boxer to receive a knighthood?	*Henry Cooper*
6	Was the father of Andre Agassi born in India, Iraq or Iran?	*Iran*
7	Who was the only Scotsman to be World Darts Champion in the 1980s?	*Jocky Wilson*
8	Which Manchester United star is the son of the rugby league professional Danny Wilson?	*Ryan Giggs*
9	Which jockey did John Hurt portray in the film *Champions*?	*Bob Champion*
10	Which Leeds United goalkeeper was a member of England's 2002 World Cup squad?	*Nigel Martyn*

Quiz 75
Question 1

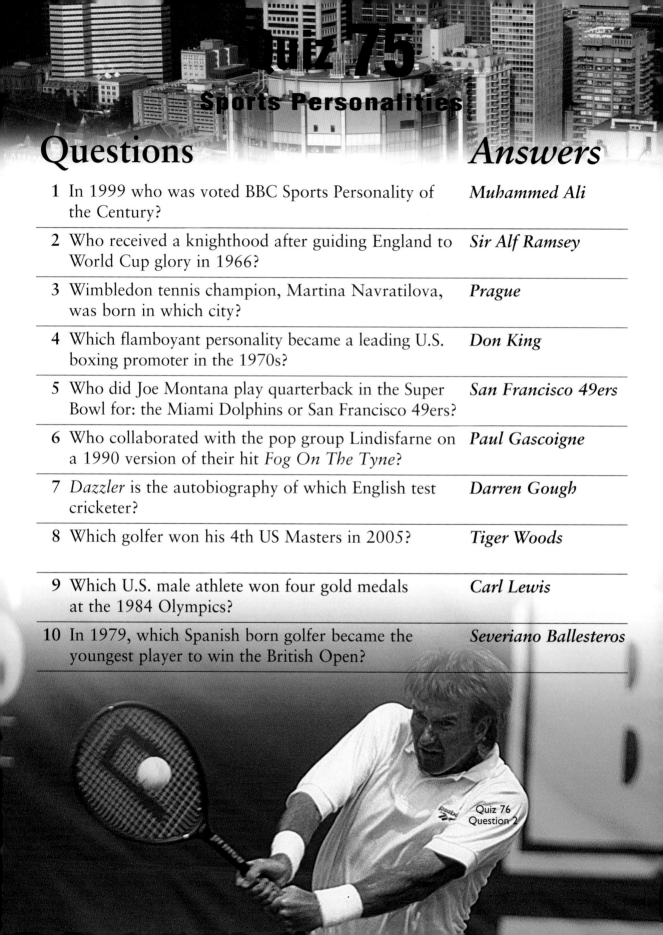

Questions

Answers

	Questions	Answers
1	In 1999 who was voted BBC Sports Personality of the Century?	*Muhammed Ali*
2	Who received a knighthood after guiding England to World Cup glory in 1966?	*Sir Alf Ramsey*
3	Wimbledon tennis champion, Martina Navratilova, was born in which city?	*Prague*
4	Which flamboyant personality became a leading U.S. boxing promoter in the 1970s?	*Don King*
5	Who did Joe Montana play quarterback in the Super Bowl for: the Miami Dolphins or San Francisco 49ers?	*San Francisco 49ers*
6	Who collaborated with the pop group Lindisfarne on a 1990 version of their hit *Fog On The Tyne*?	*Paul Gascoigne*
7	*Dazzler* is the autobiography of which English test cricketer?	*Darren Gough*
8	Which golfer won his 4th US Masters in 2005?	*Tiger Woods*
9	Which U.S. male athlete won four gold medals at the 1984 Olympics?	*Carl Lewis*
10	In 1979, which Spanish born golfer became the youngest player to win the British Open?	*Severiano Ballesteros*

Quiz 76
Question 2

Quiz 78
Touchdown Trivia

Questions	Answers
1 What name is given to the team member who directs the attacking plays of a team?	*The quarterback*
2 From which city do the Texans come?	*Houston, Texas*
3 How many players per side are on an American football team?	*Eleven*
4 In which decade was the Super Bowl first contested?	*1960s*
5 Which American football team has the last name of the Vikings?	*The Minnesota Vikings*
6 Which Spanish club has the last name of Dragons?	*The Barcelona Dragons*
7 Who were the beaten finalists in the 2001 Super Bowl?	*The New York Giants*
8 What do the initials NFL stand for?	*National Football League*
9 Which farm animal provides the last name of the Los Angeles American football team?	*Rams*
10 What name is given to the area on the pitch that attacking teams try to enter to score a touchdown?	*End zone*

Quiz 77
Question 4

Quiz 77
Touchdown Trivia

Questions	Answers
1 In minutes, what is the duration of a game of American football?	*60 minutes*
2 Which U.S. city's American football team are called the Cowboys?	*Dallas*
3 What is the name of the trophy presented to the winners of the Super Bowl?	*The Vince Lombardi Trophy*
4 Which city do the Steelers come from?	*Pittsburgh*
5 Which phrase from American football means that the defeated team has failed to score any points?	*Shut out*
6 How many points are scored for a touchdown?	*Six*
7 Which German club have the last name of Galaxy?	*The Frankfurt Galaxy*
8 In which U.S. city is The Orange Bowl?	*Miami*
9 Packers is the last name of which American football team?	*Green Bay Packers*
10 In the game of American football, what do the initials PAT stand for?	*Point after touchdown*

Quiz 78
Question 9

Quiz 80
A Sports Bag

Questions	Answers
1 What wood are cricket bats traditionally made from?	*Willow*
2 A statue of which footballer is located at the Pariwas Temple in Bangkok?	*David Beckham*
3 Who won nine Grand Prix races in the 1992 Formula One season?	*Nigel Mansell*
4 Which soccer club are nicknamed "The Hatters"?	*Luton Town*
5 Who was the first man to swim the English Channel?	*Matthew Webb*
6 In 1966 did the Brutal Bombers or The Violent Kickers win the Jamaican Football League?	*The Violent Kickers*
7 Who won Britain's only Olympic gold of the 20th century in javelin?	*Tessa Sanderson*
8 Which club did Glenn Hoddle leave to become manager of England?	*Chelsea*
9 In horse racing, what is the name of the course that stages all the Irish classics?	*The Curragh*
10 What item of soccer kit was made compulsory in 1990?	*Shin pads or shin guards*

Quiz 79
Question 1

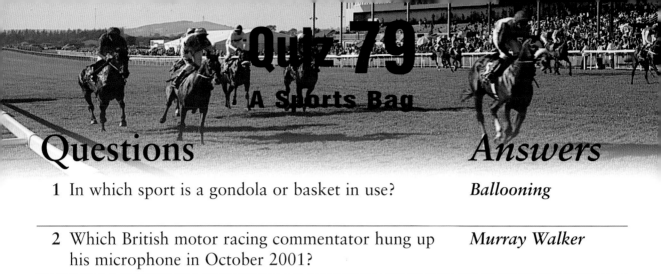

Quiz 79

A Sports Bag

Questions	Answers
1 In which sport is a gondola or basket in use?	*Ballooning*
2 Which British motor racing commentator hung up his microphone in October 2001?	*Murray Walker*
3 What is the name of the cat that was the mascot of the 2002 Commonwealth Games?	*Kit the Kat*
4 Which seaside soccer club play at Bloomfield Road?	*Blackpool*
5 Where is the All England Lawn Tennis and Croquet Club?	*Wimbledon*
6 What sport is governed by the IRF?	*Racketball*
7 In 1996, which team failed to turn up for an international soccer match with Scotland?	*Estonia*
8 Who was the first batsman to score 10,000 runs in test cricket?	*Sunil Gavaskar*
9 Which nation won the Davis Cup in tennis in 1999?	*Australia*
10 Sepp Blatter and Stanley Rous have both been presidents of which sporting organization?	*FIFA*

Quiz 80
Question 3

Quiz 82
Sport Around The World

Questions	Answers
1 In tennis, what is the name of the stadium in Paris where the French Open is contested?	*Roland Garros*
2 In which South American country is the Maracana Stadium?	*Brazil*
3 Which Spanish city hosted the 1999 World Athletics Championships?	*Seville*
4 In which country is Calgary, the venue for the 1988 Winter Olympics?	*Canada*
5 In which British city is the Millennium Stadium?	*Cardiff*
6 What connects the Olympic Games of 1896 and 2004?	*Athens*
7 Royal Troon Golf Course is in which country?	*Scotland*
8 Which soccer club left Plough Lane to share the ground at Crystal Palace?	*Wimbledon*
9 What was the venue of the only Summer Olympics of the 20th century to be held in Belgium?	*Antwerp*
10 In which county is Lord's cricket ground?	*Middlesex*

Quiz 81
Question 2

Quiz 81

Sport Around The World

Questions	Answers
1 Which British horse racing course is the largest in the world?	*Newmarket*
2 In which country is the Azteca soccer stadium?	*Mexico*
3 What is the name of the ground where Scotland play their home rugby union internationals?	*Murrayfield*
4 Which city in New Zealand hosted the Commonwealth Games in 1990?	*Auckland*
5 Which is the only British city to have hosted the Summer Olympics in the 20th century?	*London*
6 In which English county is the Belfry Golf Club?	*Warwickshire*
7 What was the first city beginning with the letter M to host the Summer Olympics?	*Mexico City*
8 In horse racing, at which course is the Irish Grand National run?	*Fairyhouse*
9 Which golf course hosted the 2002 British Open?	*Muirfield*
10 In which Italian city is the San Siro Stadium?	*Milan*

Quiz 82
Question 7

Quiz 84

Give It A Try

Questions	Answers
1 What is the nickname of Argentina's rugby union team?	*"The Pumas"*
2 In minutes, what is the duration of a rugby match?	*80 minutes*
3 How many additional points are awarded for a successful conversion kick after a try has been scored?	*Two points*
4 What kind of animal stands on top of rugby's Calcutta Cup?	*An elephant*
5 Which rugby player married the TV presenter Gabby Yorath in 2001?	*Kenny Logan*
6 Which club beat Munster to become the European Club Champions in 2002?	*Leicester*
7 Which nation were rugby union World Champions in 1995?	*South Africa*
8 Is the emblem on an England rugby union shirt a lion, a crown or a rose?	*A red rose*
9 In 1999, who won the last Five Nations rugby union international championships?	*Scotland*
10 Which English rugby league team are known as "The Chemics"?	*Widnes*

Quiz 83
Question 7

Questions

Answers

1 What is the nickname of South Africa's rugby union team?	*"Springboks"*
2 Which nation were rugby union World Champions in 1991 and 1999?	*Australia*
3 How many players from each side take part in a rugby union scrum?	*Eight*
4 Which French rugby union international won his 100th cap in 1991?	*Serge Blanco*
5 Was rugby league originally called Northern rugby, Southern rugby or Western rugby?	*Northern rugby*
6 In which Yorkshire city were the Barbarians founded?	*Bradford*
7 For which country did Jonathan Davies play international rugby?	*Wales*
8 Which rugby league club play their home matches at Central Park?	*Wigan*
9 In 1971, what changed from three to four?	*The points value of a try in rugby league*
10 Which English rugby league club are nicknamed "The Wires"?	*Warrington*

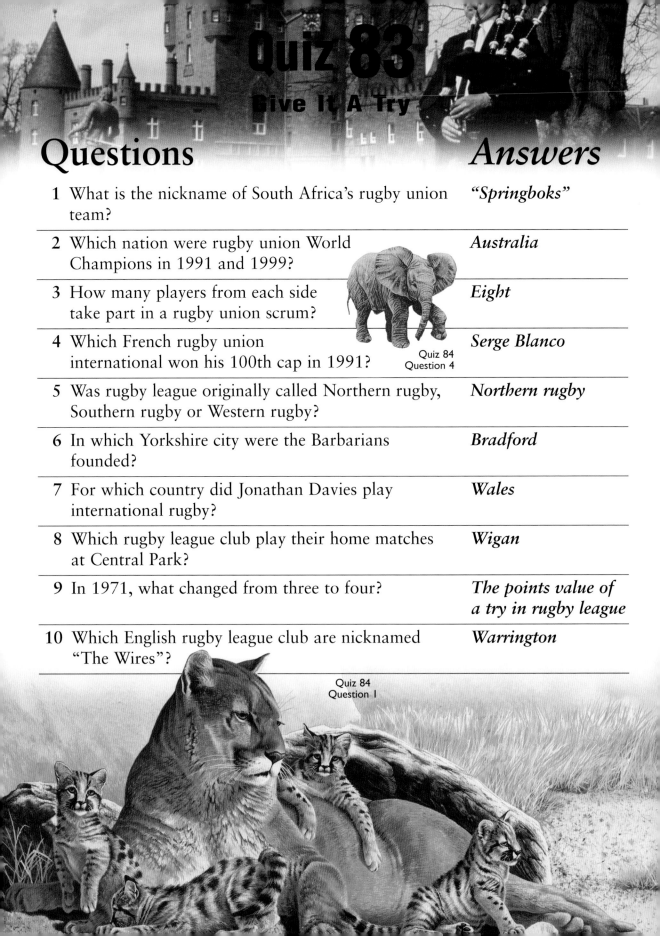

Quiz 84
Question 4

Quiz 84
Question 1

Quiz 86

A Sports Bag

Questions	Answers
1 In tenpin bowling, how many pins are on the back row?	*Four*
2 In which athletic event is a planting box used?	*Pole vault*
3 Which cricketer played soccer for Arsenal and 78 test matches for England?	*Dennis Compton*
4 Who was the first footballer to score 100 league goals for a Scottish club and an English club?	*Kenny Dalglish*
5 Which middle distance runner won Britain's only gold medal at the 1978 European Championships?	*Steve Ovett*
6 In which sport are competitors allowed six attempts from the throwing circle?	*Shot put*
7 What is the country of origin of the African athlete Haile Gebrselassie?	*Ethiopia*
8 What did the U.S. athlete Arthur Washington throw to win a gold medal at the 1999 World Athletics?	*The discus*
9 Which footballer captained Brazil to World Cup glory in 1970?	*Carlos Alberto*
10 Which former South African cricket captain died in a plane crash in 2002?	*Hanse Cronje*

Quiz 85
Question 5

Quiz 85
Question 1

Quiz 85
A Sports Bag

Questions	Answers
1 What are Blackjack, Canasta, Liverpool Rummy and Solitaire?	*Card games*
2 Who was in goal for England when Maradona scored his "Hand of God" goal?	*Peter Shilton*
3 In North America which sport cancelled its entire 2004/05 season due to a labour dispute?	*Ice hockey*
4 Which cricket ground has a Radcliffe Road end?	*Trent Bridge*
5 Bobby Fischer was the first American to be the World Champion at what?	*Chess*
6 Over how many days is the Olympic decathlon event held?	*Two*
7 FISA is the ruling body for which sport?	*Formula One motor racing*
8 At the 1999 World Athletics Championships, Abel Anton of Spain won the gold medal for which event?	*The marathon*
9 Frenchman Guy Forget played which ball sport?	*Tennis*
10 Which soccer club left Ayresome Park to move to the Riverside Stadium?	*Middlesbrough*

Quiz 86
Question 2

Questions	Answers
1 How many gold medals did Jesse Owens win at the 1936 Olympics?	*Four*
2 Which overseas snooker star is nicknamed "The Grinder"?	*Cliff Thorburn*
3 Which country is to host soccer's World Cup in 2006?	*Germany*
4 Which team won the FA Cup in 1901, 1921, 1961, 1981 and 1991?	*Tottenham Hotspur*
5 What is the maximum number of greyhounds that can run in one race?	*Eight*
6 What is West Indian cricketer Brian Lara's middle name: Charles, Edward or Andrew?	*Charles*
7 What is the last name of the brothers Rory and Tony who were teammates in England's rugby union team?	*Underwood*
8 The Fastnet Race is contested in which sport?	*Yachting*
9 A telltale, a service box and a tin can be found on the court in which racket sport?	*Squash*
10 Which was the only soccer club to win the FA Cup twice in the 1970s?	*Arsenal*

Quiz 87
Question 4

Quiz 87
A Sports Bag

Questions	Answers
1 Which country did Peter Schmeichel represent at international level?	*Denmark*
2 FINA is the ruling body for which sport?	*Swimming*
3 Which country is to host the 2002 European Nations Football Championships?	*Portugal*
4 In the world of sport, who uses a sign language known as tic–tac?	*Racetrack bookmakers*
5 Which French soccer club won their seventh league title in 2000?	*Monaco*
6 What is the last name of father Colin and son Chris, who both captained England's cricket team?	*Cowdrey*
7 What is the real first name of the decathlete Daley Thompson?	*Francis*
8 Which Monaco race was won in 2005 by Sebastien Loeb driving a Citroen Xsara?	*Monte Carlo Rally*
9 Is the game of bagatelle played on an ice rink, a table or a field?	*On a table, it is a form of bar billiards*
10 In which country was Shergar kidnapped?	*Ireland*

Quiz 88
Question 8

Quiz 90
Spot The Teams

Name the North American ice hockey teams from
their last names and the initial letters of their location

Answers

1 D................. Stars — *Dallas*

2 O................. Senators — *Ottawa*

3 C................. Flames — *Calgary*

4 C................. Avalanche — *Colorado*

5 E................. Oilers — *Edmonton*

6 P................Coyotes — *Phoenix*

7 M................. Wild — *Minnesota*

8 B................. Bruins — *Boston*

9 TB................ Lightning — *Tampa Bay*

10 P................. Flyers — *Philadelphia*

Quiz 89
Question 6

Quiz 89
Spot The Teams

Name the North American ice hockey teams from
their last names and the initial letters of their location

Answers

1 C.................... Hurricanes   *Carolina*

2 B.................... Sabres   *Buffalo*

3 C.................... Golden Seals   *California*

4 A.................... Thrashers   *Atlanta*

5 D.................... Red Wings   *Detroit*

6 C.................... Blackhawks   *Chicago*

Quiz 90
Question 1

7 C.................... Blue Jackets   *Colombus*

8 V.................... Canucks   *Vancouver*

9 NJ.................. Devils   *New Jersey*

10 F.................... Panthers   *Florida*

Quiz 90
Question 10

Quiz 92

For the Little Leaguers

Questions	Answers
1 On what surface is the Wimbledon Tennis Tournament played?	*Grass*
2 What does a boxing referee count to, to signify a knockout?	*Ten*
3 Bayern Munich F.C. are based in which country?	*Germany*
4 In cricket, what does the letter L stand for in LBW?	*Leg*
5 In which sport would you see referee Len Ganley wearing white gloves?	*Snooker*
6 Unravel the anagram – RESOLDER BALL	*Rollerblades*
7 Unravel the anagram – DONKE	*Kendo*
8 Unravel the anagram – BAT NELL	*Netball*
9 Unravel the anagram – GI SNAIL	*Sailing*
10 Unravel the anagram – HOIST NOG	*Shooting*

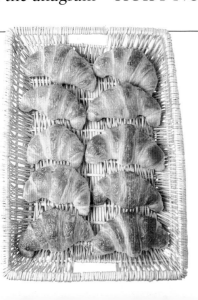

Quiz 91
Question 4

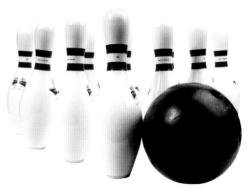

Quiz 91
Question 8

Quiz 91

For the Little Leaguers

Questions	Answers
1 Which Scottish soccer club do Rangers play in the Old Firm derby?	*Celtic*
2 In tennis, what is the score when an umpire calls deuce?	*40-40*
3 In boxing, what does the T stand for in TKO?	*Technical*
4 In which country do the soccer team Bordeaux play their home matches?	*France*
5 How many players comprise a rounders team?	*Nine*
6 Unravel the anagram – EVIL JAN	*Javelin*
7 Unravel the anagram – HARRY CE	*Archery*
8 Unravel the anagram – BIN GLOW	*Bowling*
9 Unravel the anagram – I GROWN	*Rowing*
10 Unravel the anagram – VIN DIG	*Diving*

Quiz 92
Question 6

Quiz 92
Question 9

Quiz 94
A Sports Bag

Questions	Answers
1 Eton, Rugby and Fives are all types of which handball game?	*Fives*
2 In which English city is Goodison Park soccer stadium?	*Liverpool*
3 What nationality is the golfer Colin Montgomerie?	*Scottish*
4 The Cy Young Award is presented in which U.S. sport?	*Baseball*
5 Which U.S. city's basketball team won six NBA championships in the 1990s?	*Chicago*
6 In which South American country is the world's highest golf course?	*Peru*
7 In which town did Sir Francis Drake reputedly finish a game of bowls before defeating the Armada?	*Plymouth*
8 With which sport do we associate the U.S. group The Beach Boys?	*Surfing*
9 What is the name of the trophy presented to the winning nation of rugby union's World Cup?	*William Webb Ellis Trophy*
10 Was the man who instigated the modern Olympics British, French or Greek?	*French (Baron de Coubertin)*

Quiz 93
Question 5

Quiz 93
Question 1

Quiz 93

A Sports Bag

Questions	Answers
1 Which former Wimbledon champion partnered Tony Blair in a charity tennis match in June 2002?	*Pat Cash*
2 Which European country won the third place play-off in the 1974 and 1982 soccer World Cups?	*Poland*
3 Which British motor racing track is built on an old airfield once used for RAF training?	*Silverstone*
4 In cricket, what G word is an alternative name for a bowling delivery that is also called a Bosie?	*Googly*
5 Which event did TV presenter Gabby Logan participate in at the Commonwealth Games as a teenager?	*Gymnastics*
6 In horseracing, does the term double carpet signify betting odds of 33-1, 66-1 or 100-1?	*33-1*
7 Which hero of classical mythology is also the name of the soccer team based in Amsterdam?	*Ajax*
8 What type of sword is used exclusively in women's fencing?	*Foil*
9 What is the most northerly country that hosted the soccer World Cup in the 20th century?	*Sweden*
10 Which Dutch tennis player won the men's singles at Wimbledon in 1996?	*Richard Krajicek*

Quiz 94
Question 8

Quiz 96

Let's Have A Ball!

Questions	Answers
1 In table tennis, after how many points do players change serve?	*Five*
2 In which game do you use a tolley?	*Marbles*
3 What is longer: a baseball bat or a tennis racket?	*A baseball bat*
4 Who captained England's rugby union international team in 2002?	*Martin Johnson*
5 What would the total break be if a snooker player potted seven reds and seven blacks?	*56*
6 Aged 42, which Cameroon striker was the oldest player to score a goal in the World Cup finals?	*Roger Milla*
7 What did the basketball legend Lew Alcindor change his name to?	*Kareem Abdul-Jabbar*
8 Which sport, popular in Ireland, is played using a ball called a *sliothar*?	*Hurling*
9 Who was the No. 1 seed in the women's singles at the 2002 Wimbledon Tournament?	*Venus Williams*
10 Which nation does England play when contesting the Calcutta Cup?	*Scotland*

Quiz 95
Question 5

Quiz 95
Question 10

Quiz 95

Let's Have A Ball!

Questions	Answers
1 Which sport uses balls with a blue dot, a white dot, a red dot and a yellow dot?	*Squash*
2 What is the maximum number of clubs a golfer is allowed to take onto the course?	*14*
3 What type of ball has three holes and weighs 7.25 kg?	*A tenpin bowling ball*
4 In 2006, which country won the inaugural World Baseball Championships, beating Cuba in the final?	*Japan*
5 On which Mediterranean Island was the snooker star Tony Drago born?	*Malta*
6 Which soccer club finished second in the 2002 Premier League in England?	*Liverpool*
7 Who captained the England cricket team on their 2002 tour of Sri Lanka?	*Nasser Hussain*
8 Which game developed from wooden balls being hit through hoops of willow?	*Croquet*
9 Who was No. 1 seed in the men's singles at the 2002 Wimbledon Championships?	*Lleyton Hewitt*
10 Which golfer won the U.S. Open in 2002?	*Tiger Woods*

Quiz 96
Question 3

Questions	Answers
1 In which event did Shelley Rudman win a silver medal for Britain at the 2006 Winter Olympics?	*Bob skeleton*
2 Which item of equestrian clothing is named after the Indian city where they originated?	*Jodhpurs*
3 Who did David Beckham kick, before being sent off, in a 1998 World Cup match against Argentina?	*Diego Simeone*
4 Who was sacked as England's rugby union captain in 1995, but was reinstated a few days later?	*Will Carling*
5 On a yacht, what shape is a lateen sail?	*Triangular*
6 What type of canoe is a palindrome?	*Kayak (spells the same both ways)*
7 What do weightlifters put on their hands to improve their grip?	*Powder*
8 Which horse won the 2002 Grand National?	*Bindaree*
9 Which British tennis player won the women's singles at Wimbledon in 1969?	*Ann Jones*
10 A matador uses an *estoque*. What is it?	*A sword*

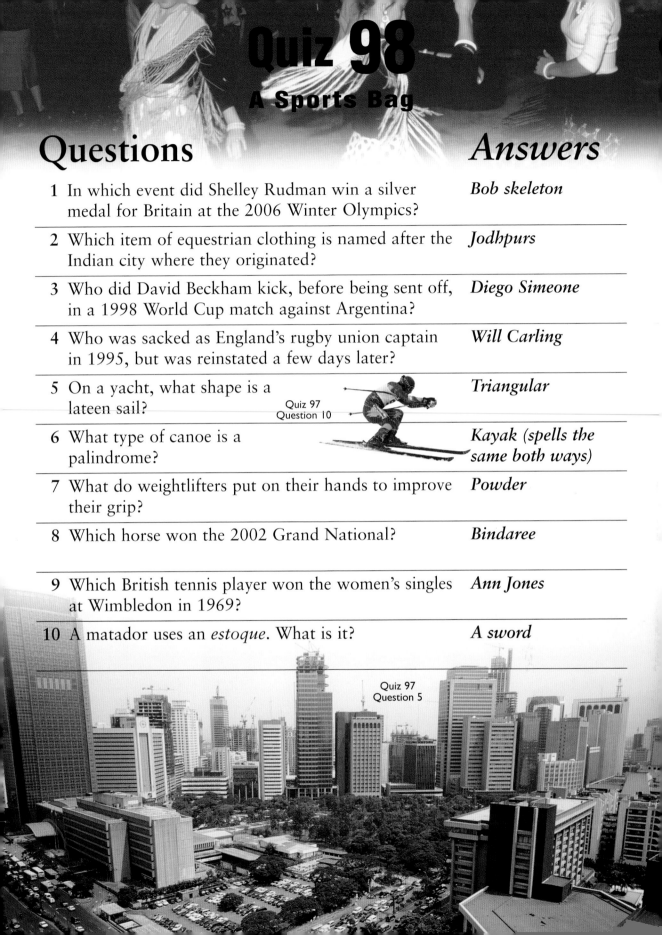

Quiz 97
Question 10

Quiz 97
Question 5

Quiz 97
A Sports Bag

Questions	Answers
1 At which racecourse is the St. Leger run?	*Doncaster*
2 Which Scottish born player was crowned World Snooker Champion in 1998?	*John Higgins*
3 How many World Cups did England participate in the 1970s?	*Only one, in 1970*
4 What was the name of the IBM computer that beat World Chess Champion Gary Kasparov in 1997?	*Deep Blue*
5 In which country was the boxing match called the "Thrilla In Manila" between Ali and Frazier fought?	*Philippines*
6 Over what distance did British athlete Ann Packer win an Olympic gold medal in the 1960s?	*800 m*
7 In baseball, does the home side or the away side always bat first?	*The away side*
8 Which American football team won the American Superbowl in 2006?	*Pittsburgh Steelers*
9 In which country is the Santa Ponsa golf course?	*Spain*
10 Contested in Switzerland, what type of race is the Inferno?	*A downhill ski race*

Quiz 98
Question 7

Quiz 100
A Sports Bag

Questions	Answers
1 Which piece of sporting equipment has a maximum length of 96.5 cm and a maximum width of 10.8 cm?	*A cricket bat*
2 Which country were the appropriate hosts of the Olympic games when Judo made its debut?	*Japan*
3 Which city won the vote to host the 2008 Summer Olympics?	*Beijing*
4 How many hurdles does each runner negotiate in a 110 m hurdle race?	*Ten*
5 Which sport begins with a storke-off?	*Bandy*
6 Cobi, the official mascot of the 1992 Olympics, was what type of animal?	*A dog*
7 On what shape of pitch is Australian rules football played?	*Oval*
8 For which soccer club was Kevin Phillips the leading scorer in the Premiership in the 1999/2000 season?	*Sunderland*
9 What did Thomas Burgess become the second man to do in September 1911?	*Swim the English Channel*
10 Which nation was beaten in the final of the 1994 soccer World Cup on a penalty shoot out?	*Italy*

Quiz 99
Question 9

Quiz 99
Question 10

Quiz 99

A Sports Bag

Questions	Answers
1 Who did Celtic beat in the final when they became the first British soccer club to win the European Cup?	*Inter Milan*
2 What first was achieved by Edmund Hillary and Tenzing Norgay in May 1953?	*The first to climb Mount Everest*
3 In tennis, what is the score in a set when the tiebreak comes into play?	*6-6*
4 On what side of the yacht is the starboard side?	*Right side*
5 In which equestrian event did Bonfire win gold at the 2000 Olympics?	*Dressage*
6 In the 1990s, what was won by Benny the Dip, Oath and Dr Devious?	*The Epsom Derby*
7 What nationality was the long distance runner Ingrid Kristiansen?	*Norwegian*
8 Johnny Weissmuller went on to play Tarzan after winning five Olympic golds in which sport?	*Swimming*
9 Which nation reached a score of 952 for 6 declared in a 1998 cricket test match against India?	*Sri Lanka*
10 Who won 108 caps for England from 1962 to 1973?	*Bobby Moore*

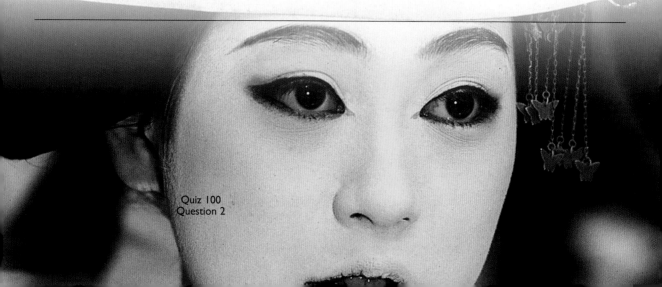

Quiz 100
Question 2

Quiz 102
Howzat!

Questions	Answers
1 Grace Road is the home of which county cricket club?	*Leicestershire*
2 What does the M stand for in MCC?	*Marylebone*
3 In 2005 who became the first bowler to take 600 Test wickets?	*Shane Warne*
4 Which West Indian batsman scored a record 375 runs in a test match against England?	*Brian Lara*
5 What is the criminal nickname of Nottinghamshire County Cricket Club?	*"The Outlaws"*
6 Who captained England on their controversial Bodyline Tour of Australia in the 1930s?	*Douglas Jardine*
7 What name is given to an illegal delivery in cricket?	*No ball*
8 Which mythical bird provides the last name of Yorkshire County Club in the National League?	*Phoenix*
9 Which member of England's 1966 soccer World Cup winning team played county cricket?	*Geoff Hurst*
10 Eaton Road, Hove, is the home of which county cricket club?	*Sussex*

Quiz 101
Question 5

Quiz 101

Howzat!

Questions	Answers
1 Who captained the England women's cricket team for 11 years from 1966?	*Rachel Heyhoe-Flint*
2 What is the name of the test cricket ground in Nottingham?	*Trent Bridge*
3 What is an umpire signalling when raising an open hand above the head?	*A bye*
4 Who was the first bowler to take 350 test wickets for England?	*Ian Botham*
5 Which Indian test cricketer is nicknamed "The Bengal Tiger"?	*Sourav Ganguly*
6 Which former test cricketer went on to become the Bishop of Liverpool?	*David Sheppard*
7 Which county cricket team are known as "The Crusaders"?	*Middlesex*
8 Brothers Hanif, Sadiq, Wazir and Mustaq Mohammed all play test cricket for which country?	*Pakistan*
9 Which monarch made cricket illegal in Britain in 1447?	*Edward IV*
10 Which county cricket team play at home at Sophia Gardens in Cardiff?	*Glamorgan*

Quiz 102
Question 8

Quiz 102
Question 4

Quiz 104
A Sports Bag

Questions	Answers
1 What M word is the name given to the art of knotting string and cord into patterns?	*Macramé*
2 At the start of a game of draughts, how many squares on the board are not occupied by pieces?	*40*
3 Which fellow Swede became Sven Goran Eriksson's assistant manager for the England team?	*Tord Grip*
4 Which gold medallist carried the Union Jack in the opening ceremony of the 2000 Sydney Olympics?	*Steve Redgrave*
5 Which Yorkshire man was the first bowler to take 300 test wickets for England?	*Freddie Trueman*
6 What did the Empire Games change its name to?	*The Commonwealth Games*
7 Which insect provides the nickname for Watford F.C.?	*Hornets*
8 What card game is also the name of a floating bridge?	*Pontoon*
9 In which game do players start with 501 subtracting their score after each turn until one of them reaches 0?	*Darts*
10 Name the politician who captained Britain's 1971 Admirals Cup sailing team?	*Edward Heath*

Quiz 103
Question 3

Quiz 103
Question 1

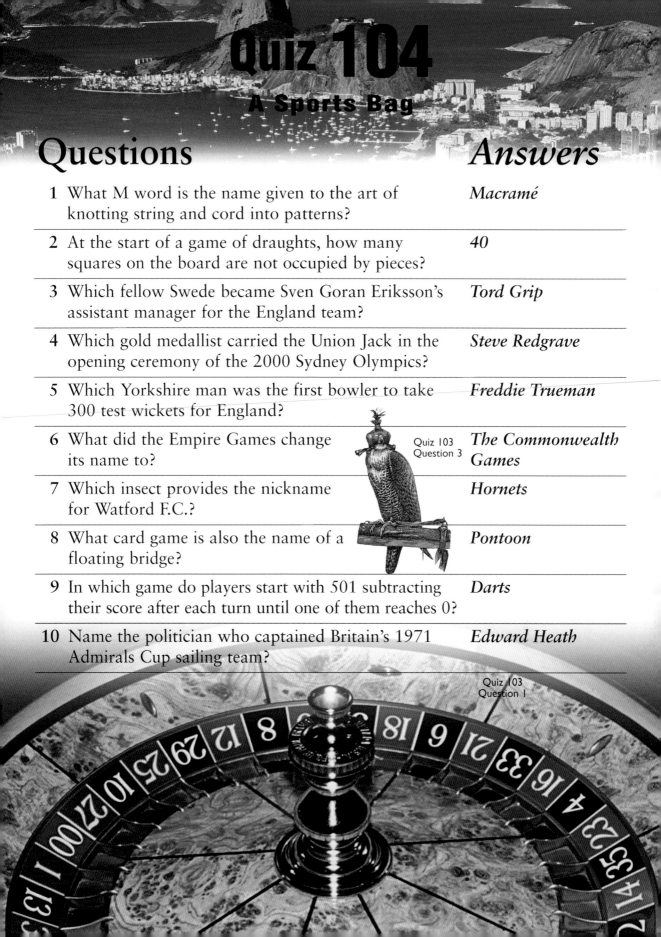

Quiz 103

A Sports Bag

Questions	Answers
1 Frenchman Blaise Bascal was the inventor of which gaming device?	*The roulette wheel*
2 In which year did synchronised swimming make its Olympic debut?	*1984*
3 What name is given to the practice of training hawks?	*Falconry*
4 How did the boxer Rocky Marciano die?	*In a plane crash*
5 How many members are there in a women's lacrosse team?	*12 (ten in a men's)*
6 Mark Hughes and Gary Lineker both played for which Spanish soccer club?	*Barcelona*
7 What is the name of Glasgow Rangers' ground?	*Ibrox Stadium*
8 At the 1966 soccer World Cup, which nation entered the tournament as defending World Champions?	*Brazil*
9 Tennis star Kim Clijsters hails from which European country?	*Belgium*
10 Which sport was originally called kitten ball?	*Softball*

Quiz 104
Question 9

Quiz 104
Question 7

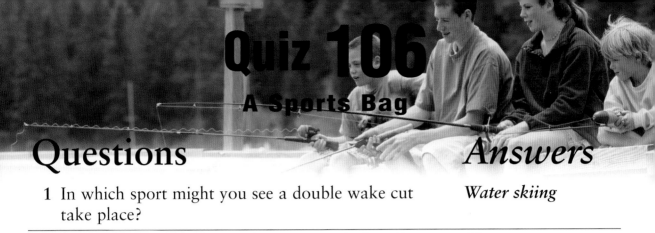

Quiz 106
A Sports Bag

Questions	Answers
1 In which sport might you see a double wake cut take place?	*Water skiing*
2 To make a perfect score of 300 in tenpin bowling, how many successive strikes must be registered?	*12*
3 Which Scottish driver won the British Grand Prix five times in the 1960s?	*Jim Clark*
4 To a golfer, what is a nervous disability affecting the putting?	*The yips*
5 On a chessboard what are the files?	*The vertical rows*
6 On which flag are the words Citius, Altius, Fortius written?	*The Olympic flag*
7 What do the initials ICC stand for in the world of sport?	*International Cricket Conference*
8 When taking a snooker shot, how many feet must the player keep on the floor?	*At least one foot*
9 Which sport took its name from the Tibetan word for ball?	*Polo*
10 Who partnered Martina Navratilova to consecutive Wimbledon doubles titles from 1981 to 1984?	*Pam Shriver*

Quiz 105
Question 4

Quiz 105
Question 1

Quiz 105

A Sports Bag

Questions	Answers
1 Who was Wimbledon men's singles champion in 1976?	*Bjorn Borg*
2 Which pop star cried at Wembley in 1984 after Everton beat Watford in the FA Cup?	*Elton John*
3 How many railway stations are there on a Monopoly board?	*Four*
4 What has a racehorse done if it has spread a plate?	*Lost a shoe*
5 What is the middle division on a backgammon board called?	*The bar*
6 What do the initials TP signify to an archer?	*Target practice*
7 In which country is the world's oldest golf course?	*Scotland (St. Andrews)*
8 At which sports ground do spectators watch the action from the Mound Stand and the Warner Stand?	*Lord's Cricket Ground*
9 In which Texan city is the Astrodome Stadium?	*Houston*
10 What pastime is enjoyed by a piscatologist?	*Fishing*

Quiz 106
Question 6

Quiz 106
Question 1

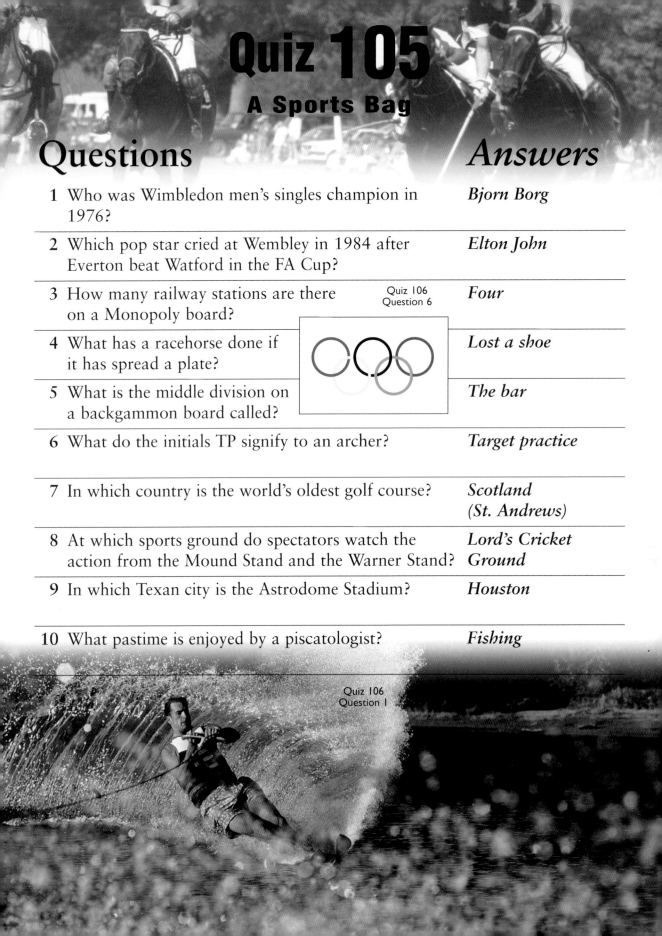

Quiz 108

Baseball Bonanza & Name the Team

Questions	Answers
1 How many umpires officiate over a baseball game?	*Four*
2 Which great player was also known as the "Sultan of Swat"?	*Babe Ruth*
3 In baseball, what is the warm–up area for batters and pitchers known as?	*The bullpen*
4 What is called when a batter swings and misses the ball thrown by a pitcher?	*A strike*
5 The Los Angeles Dodgers were previously known as what?	*Brooklyn Dodgers*
6 Name the team – M........ Twins	*Minnesota*
7 Name the team – Atlanta B.....	*Braves*
8 Name the team – A...... Diamondbacks	*Arizona*
9 Name the team – St. L.... Cardinals	*St. Louis*
10 Name the team – M........ Braves	*Milwaukee*

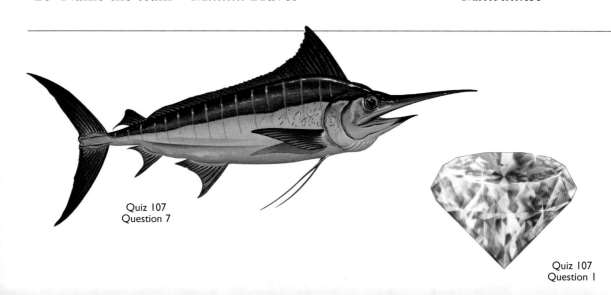

Quiz 107
Question 7

Quiz 107
Question 1

Quiz 107

Baseball Bonanza & Name the Team

	Questions	Answers
1	What name is given to the area of the baseball field formed by the four bases?	*The diamond*
2	In which decade was baseball's Hall Of Fame founded?	*1930s*
3	What is the name of the area where a batter stands to receive the ball?	*Home base*
4	What is the area called where players, subs and managers sit when not in play?	*The dug out*
5	What is the keystone the alternative name for in baseball?	*The second base*
6	Name the team – S... D.... Padres	*San Diego*
7	Name the team – Florida M......	*Marlins*
8	Name the team – B........ Orioles	*Baltimore*
9	Name the team – C........ Reds	*Cincinnati*
10	Name the team – B....... Dodgers	*Brooklyn*

Quiz 108
Question 2

Quiz 110

A Sports Bag

Questions	Answers
1 Which Scottish soccer club is an anagram of BRAT ON MUD?	*Dumbarton*
2 England managers Alf Ramsey, Terry Venables and Glenn Hoddle all played for which team?	*Tottenham Hotspur*
3 Who won the snooker World Championships on 15 occasions in the 20th century?	*Joe Davis*
4 Which Scottish soccer league team have their ground in England?	*Berwick Rangers*
5 What are table tennis balls made from?	*Celluloid*
6 Which jockey nicknamed "The Choirboy" won the Derby on Shergar?	*Walter Swinburn*
7 Which of the Olympic rings represents Australia?	*The green ring*
8 At the BBC Sports Personality of the Year Awards of 2002, who was the only woman on the shortlist of six?	*Ellen Macarthur*
9 Which nation's national anthem is played at the closing ceremony of the Olympic games?	*Greece*
10 Who was named Player of the Tournament for the 2005 Ashes?	*Andrew "Freddie" Flintoff*

Quiz 109
Question 10

Quiz 109

A Sports Bag

Questions	Answers
1 Which Scottish soccer club is an anagram of NORMAL KICK?	*Kilmarnock*
2 In which country is the Bellerive Oval cricket ground?	*Australia*
3 On a golf green, what is known as the borrow?	*The slope of the green*
4 Who was the first footballer to be voted BBC Sports Personality of the Year?	*Bobby Moore*
5 In which decade did India play their first cricket test match?	*The 1930s*
6 Which of the Olympic rings represents Europe?	*The blue ring*
7 Which team finished bottom of the English Premiership in the 2001/2002 season?	*Leicester City*
8 Who was the last snooker player in the 20th century to retain the World Snooker title?	*Stephen Hendry*
9 Which tennis star had a cameo appearance in the Jim Carrey film *Me, Myself And Irene*?	*Anna Kournikova*
10 Throughout the 1990s, which cricketer scored the most test runs for England?	*Alec Stewart*

Quiz 110
Question 8

Quiz 112
Total Trivia

Questions	Answers
1 Which sport was prohibited by King Edward III in 1365 because of its excessive violence?	*Soccer*
2 What sport did Errol Flynn represent Australia in at the 1928 Olympics?	*Boxing*
3 In 1997, whose 147 break at the World Snooker Championships took 320 seconds to clear the table?	*Ronnie O'Sullivan*
4 Which swimmer at the 2000 Olympics only learned to swim in the year before the Games?	*Eric Moussambani*
5 In which position did Pope John Paul II play for the amateur soccer club, Wotsyla?	*Goalkeeper*
6 Which player recorded the fastest ever tennis service in the 20th century?	*Greg Rusedski*
7 Which top box office film star is a former Austrian Junior Weightlifting Champion?	*Arnold Schwarzenegger*
8 A depression made in the snow by a skier who has fallen backwards is known as what?	**A sitzmark**
9 At a 2000 auction at Christies in London, whose No. 10 shirt sold for £91,750?	*Geoff Hurst's*
10 At which sport did Australia beat New Zealand 58-0 in March 1987?	*Ice hockey*

Quiz 111
Question 6

Quiz 111
Total Trivia

Questions	Answers
1 Which boxer's figure in the Hollywood Wax Museum was moved next to the figure of Hannibal Lecter?	*Mike Tyson*
2 Which country won badminton's World Championship a record 12 times in the 20th century?	*Indonesia*
3 Which 2005 world championships saw Spain lift the gold medal, Croatia the silver and France the bronze?	*Handball*
4 How many Olympic gold medals did the swimmer Mark Spitz win in his career?	*Nine*
5 Which future comedy actor competed in the 1980 Oxford and Cambridge boat race?	*Hugh Lawrie*
6 Who won 20 Wimbledon titles between 1961 and 1979?	*Billie Jean King*
7 In which event did the future General George Patton compete in the 1912 Olympics?	*Pentathlon*
8 At 17 years and 41 days old, who was the youngest player to play in a World Cup final match?	*Norman Whiteside of N. Ireland*
9 Who won a rowing gold medal at the 1924 Olympics and wrote a babycare book in 1938?	*Dr. Benjamin Spock*
10 Who earned $9,188,321 in prize money in the year 2000?	*Tiger Woods*

Quiz 112
Question 7

Quiz 114

It's a Knockout!

Questions	Answers
1 Who was the first boxer to win world titles in six different weight categories?	*Thomas Hearns*
2 In which European country was Joe Bugner born?	*Hungary*
3 Which corner of the ring must a boxer stand in after knocking down an opponent?	*A neutral corner*
4 Who did Sugar Ray Leonard name himself after?	*Sugar Ray Robinson*
5 What was worn for the first time in a boxing bout in a 1892 fight between Jim Corbett and John L. Sullivan?	*Boxing gloves*
6 What does a referee count up to when giving a boxer a standing count?	*Eight*
7 In professional boxing, which weight category has an upper limit of 67 kg?	*Welterweight*
8 In which film did Robert DeNiro play the middleweight boxer Jake La Motta?	**Raging Bull**
9 By what title was John Sholto Douglas also known?	*The Marquess of Queensbury*
10 Is a bolo a jab, an uppercut punch or a left hook?	*An uppercut punch*

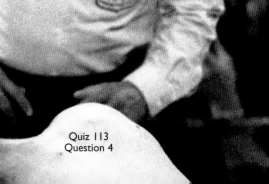

Quiz 113
Question 4

Quiz 113

It's a Knockout!

Questions	Answers
1 In 1985, which Irishman defeated Eusibio Pedroza to become World Featherweight Champion?	*Barry McGuigan*
2 Who did Muhammed Ali lose his world title to in 1978?	*Leon Spinks*
3 Who was the last boxer in the 20th century to defeat Lennox Lewis?	*Hasim Rahman*
4 Who did Muhammed Ali beat to win the world title for the second time?	*George Foreman*
5 Which former heavyweight champion died in 2006 aged 71?	*Floyd Patterson*
6 Who was the longest reigning heavyweight champion of the 20th century?	*Joe Louis*
7 Rocky Marciano retired undefeated after how many fights, was it 48, 49 or 50?	49
8 In 1992, which country lifted a long-standing ban on professional boxing?	*Soviet Union*
9 Which heavyweight boxer appeared as himself in the film *Rocky*?	*Joe Frazier*
10 What kind of birds did Mike Tyson keep as pets when he was a youngster?	*Pigeons*

Quiz 114
Question 8

Questions

Answers

1 Which Argentinean footballer scored for Tottenham Hotspur in the 1981 FA Cup final?

Ricardo Villa

2 What sport became professional in England in May 1996?

Rugby union

3 What is the fastest creature that is raced in sport?

Pigeons

4 In which sport could you see a barani, seat drop or Randolph?

Quiz 115
Question 3

Trampolining

5 Which female long distance runner was awarded the MBE in 2002?

Paula Radcliffe

6 In which U.S. state did surfing originate?

Hawaii

7 Which Scottish soccer club took its name from a ballroom that was frequented by the players?

Heart of Midlothian

8 What was the title of the film in which Bill Murray blew up a golf course?

Caddyshack

9 What nationality was the tennis hero Rene Lacoste?

French

10 Who was the first player from Thailand to compete in the World Snooker Championships?

James Wattana

Quiz 115
Question 7

Quiz 115

A Sports Bag

Questions	Answers
1 What is the only sport that represents a letter in the NATO phonetic alphabet?	*Golf*
2 Who won Olympic gold medals for the long jump in 1984, 1988 and 1992?	*Carl Lewis*
3 In which country did the card game bridge originate?	*Turkey*
4 Which four words are depicted above the gates at Anfield, the home of Liverpool F.C.?	*You'll Never Walk Alone*
5 Which race was originally called The Liverpool Steeple Chase?	*The Grand National*
6 Who added over 55 cm to the world long jump record in 1968?	*Bob Beamon*
7 In which water sport is the Harmsworth Trophy contested?	*Powerboat racing*
8 Royal and Woolwich were formerly part of the name of which London soccer club?	*Arsenal*
9 In which country was the tennis star Monica Seles born?	*Yugoslavia*
10 Which sport featured in the film *White Men Can't Jump*?	*Basketball*

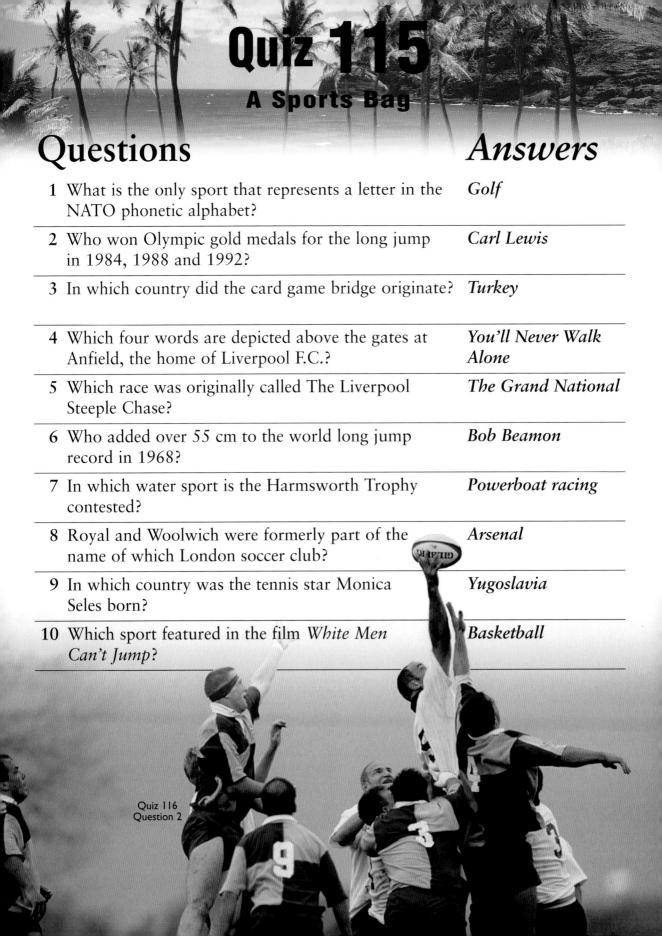

Quiz 116
Question 2

Quiz 118

For the Little Leaguers

Questions	Answers
1 Which medal is awarded for third place in an Olympic final?	*Bronze*
2 What name is given to a golfer's assistant who carries the clubs?	*The caddy*
3 What is passed from runner to runner in a relay race?	*A baton*
4 Which country, that shares its name with a bird, was knocked out of the 2002 World Cup semi-finals?	*Turkey*
5 In which Scottish city do Celtic play their home matches?	*Glasgow*
6 Which country's rugby league team are nicknamed "The Kangaroos"?	*Australia*
7 INN SET is an anagram of which sport?	*Tennis*
8 What B word is the name given to the two pieces of wood that are placed on top of cricket wickets?	*Bails*
9 Who did Manchester United play in the only FA Cup final of the 20th century contested by two Uniteds?	*Newcastle United*
10 Which duo released the 2002 World Cup song, "We're On The Ball"?	*Ant and Dec*

Quiz 117
Question 4

Quiz 117

For the Little Leaguers

Questions	Answers
1 What kind of race is the Tour de France?	*Cycling*
2 In which sport do competitors travel on a skeleton?	*Tobogganing*
3 In a soccer penalty shootout, how many penalties does each side take before sudden death begins?	*Five*
4 In which sport would you expect to see Frankie Dettori wearing silks?	*Horseracing*
5 In which city do Aston Villa play their home matches?	*Birmingham*
6 Describe the flag that is waved in Formula One racing when a driver crosses the finishing line.	*Black and white chequered*
7 How many players are in a beach volleyball team?	*Two*
8 What is the nationality of the soccer boss who managed England's 2002 Premier League Champions?	*French, Arsene Wenger of Arsenal*
9 At which horse and ball sport have Princes William and Harry been teammates of their father Prince Charles?	*Polo*
10 Which soccer team known as "The Hammers" play in claret and blue shirts?	*West Ham United*

Quiz 118
Question 8

Quiz 118
Question 3

Quiz 119
Horsing Around

Questions	Answers
1 By what name is Jennifer Susan Harvey better known in the world of horseracing?	*Jenny Pitman*
2 Which nation won the Team Show Jumping event at the 2000 Sydney Olympics?	*Germany*
3 Who trained Street Cry to win the Dubai World Cup race in 2002?	*Saeed bin Suroor*
4 In which sport would you encounter the Devil's Dyke and Derby Bank at Hickstead?	*Showjumping*
5 In the United States, what type of race is the Hambletonian?	*A trotting race*
6 In which century was the Epsom Derby first run?	*18th century*
7 What P word is the name of the place where racehorses congregate before the start of a race?	*The paddock*
8 What is a racehorse that has yet to win a race called?	*A maiden*
9 What is the name of the road that is crossed by the horses in the Aintree Grand National?	*Melling Road*
10 What is the minimum age at which a horse is allowed to compete in Olympic equestrian events?	*Seven years old*

Quiz 120
Question 3

LONGCHAMP

Questions

Answers

1 What birthday is shared by all racehorses in the Northern hemisphere?

January 1

2 What N word is the name given to a handicap horse race for two year olds?

Nursery

3 At which course is the Prix de L'Arc de Triomphe run?

Longchamps

4 What is the name of the controlling body for flat racing in Britain?

The Jockey Club

5 At which race course was a statue of Gold Cup winner Best Mate unveiled in March 2006?

Cheltenham

6 In show jumping, how many refusals is a rider and horse allowed before disqualification?

Three

7 What happened to delay the 1997 Grand National?

A bomb scare

8 Which U.S. jockey was nicknamed "The Kentucky Kid" and became Champion jockey in the U.K. in 1987?

Steve Cauthen

9 What was the name of the first woman to compete in the Grand National?

Charlotte Brew

10 The Stewards Cup and The Sussex Stakes are contested at which glorious racecourse?

Goodwood

Quiz 119
Question 4

Quiz 122
A Sports Bag

Questions	Answers
1 Petra Felke was the first woman to throw what over 80 m (87.5 yards)?	*The javelin*
2 Tony Alcock and David Bryant are both associated with which sport?	*Bowls*
3 Who was knighted in 1967 after sailing around the world in a yacht called *Gypsy Moth IV*?	*Sir Francis Chichester*
4 In chess, which piece moves with a rook in a move known as castling?	*The king*
5 What is the lowest boxing weight category?	*Strawweight*
6 Which former Wimbledon champion was knocked out of the 2002 tournament by an unseeded Swiss?	*Pete Sampras*
7 Who was the first West Indian cricketer to play in 100 test matches?	*Clive Lloyd*
8 Which sport is sometimes described as "bowls on ice"?	*Curling*
9 At which sport do the Oxford and Cambridge universities compete for the Bowring Bowl?	*Rugby union*
10 In 1980, which communist country became the first to win the Davis Cup in tennis?	*Czechoslovakia*

Quiz 121
Question 7

Quiz 121
A Sports Bag

Questions	Answers
1 Which former Italian international footballer was sacked as manager of Watford F.C. in 2002?	*Gianluca Vialli*
2 For which county cricket team did Geoff Boycott play?	*Yorkshire*
3 What F word is the name given to a pigeon breeder or racer?	*A fancier*
4 In a triathlon event, is swimming, running or cycling the last discipline?	*Running*
5 On which island was the cricketer Sir Garfield Sobers born?	*Barbados*
6 Which Olympic gold medallist of the 1996 games went on to become a star in the World Wrestling Federation?	*Kurt Angle*
7 In which sport was the Walker Cup named after George Herbert Walker?	*Golf*
8 In rugby union, what number shirt is usually worn by the outside half?	*Ten*
9 Which athlete did Ian Charleston play in the film *Chariots Of Fire*?	*Eric Liddell*
10 Who was the only U.S. born winner of the ladies singles at Wimbledon in the 1990s?	*Lindsay Davenport*

Quiz 122
Question 6

Quiz 124
A Sports Bag

Questions	Answers
1 The Roodee is the name of the horseracing course in which city?	*Chester*
2 What do the initials W.T.A. stand for in the world of sport?	*Women's Tennis Association*
3 In which game do players employ the Sicilian manoeuvre?	*Chess*
4 Why did Manchester United play their home matches at Maine Road in the 1940s?	*Old Trafford had been bombed*
5 Which British tennis star wrote an autobiography entitled *Courting Triumph*?	*Virginia Wade*
6 Which American football team won the most Super Bowls in the 1980s?	*San Francisco 49ers*
7 Despite qualifying for the 1950 World Cup, why were India banned from competing?	*They refused to wear boots*
8 Which animal gives its name to an ice-skating manoeuvre?	*The camel*
9 What type of sporting hall has a name that literally means naked exercise?	*Gymnasium*
10 In tennis, what is faster, a grass court or a clay court?	*Grass court*

Quiz 123
Question 4

Quiz 123

A Sports Bag

Questions	Answers
1 How many players comprise a Canadian football team?	*12*
2 In 1970, which horse won the St. Leger, the 2000 Guineas and the Derby?	*Nijinsky*
3 Who was crowned World Snooker Champion in 2006?	*Graeme Dott*
4 In which sport do competitors race head to head in an event called the parallel giant slalom?	*Snowboarding*
5 At which sport have the Whittaker brothers, Michael and John, represented Great Britain?	*Show jumping*
6 Which Paralympian was created a Dame in 2004?	*Tanni Grey-Thompson*
7 What form of bowling is played on a green with a raised middle area?	*Crown green bowling*
8 Former Olympian Geoff Capes is a leading breeder of which popular pets?	*Budgies*
9 Which popular children's game was called nuts in Ancient Rome?	*Marbles*
10 Which Formula One racing team have an emblem in the form of a prancing horse?	*Ferrari*

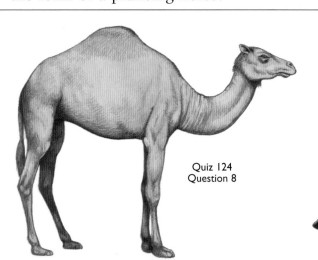

Quiz 124
Question 8

Quiz 124
Question 9

Quiz 126
A Round Of Golf

Questions	Answers
1 What number of golfing iron is a wedge?	*A number ten iron*
2 Which Spanish player won the U.S. Masters in 1999?	*Jose Maria Olazabel*
3 Over how many holes are major tournaments played?	*72 holes*
4 In which English county is the Royal Birkdale golf course?	*Lancashire*
5 In golf what is a bogey?	*A score of one over par on a hole*
6 Which British golfer won the U.S. Masters in 1991?	*Ian Woosnam*
7 Who is the youngest golfer to complete golf's Grand Slam?	*Tiger Woods*
8 Who was the only golfer in the 20th century with a double-barrelled surname to win the British Open?	*Ian Baker-Finch*
9 Which Tom won three British Opens in the 1980s?	*Tom Watson*
10 The first golf balls to be made were filled with which substance?	*Feathers*

Quiz 125
Question 5

Quiz 125
Question 7

Quiz 125
A Round Of Golf

Questions	Answers
1 Which golfing team tournament first took place in Massachusetts in 1927?	*The Ryder Cup*
2 At which British golf course do players encounter The Valley of Sin?	*St. Andrews*
3 Who was the first British golfer to win the U.S. Open after World War II?	*Tony Jacklin*
4 What D word is the alternative name for a No. 1 wood?	*Driver*
5 The Ridgewood golf course is in which U.S. state?	*New Jersey*
6 Which British golfer won the British Open in 1999?	*Paul Lawrie*
7 Which South African player won the U.S. Open in 1997?	*Ernie Els*
8 What do the initials PGA stand for?	*Professional Golfers Association*
9 Who won the British Open in 2001?	*David Duval*
10 In 2005, which Scottish golfer topped the European Order of Merit?	*Colin Montgomerie*

Quiz 126
Question 2

Quiz 128

For the Little Leaguers

Questions	Answers
1 What nationality is the soccer manager Alex Ferguson?	*Scottish*
2 What mechanical animal is chased by greyhounds in a greyhound race?	*The hare*
3 Is a thrown forward pass allowed in rugby?	*No*
4 Which singer starred with Tom Hanks and Geena Davis in the film "A League of Their Own"?	*Madonna*
5 In snooker, which ball has a value of 1 point when potted?	*The red ball*
6 In the board game *Scrabble*, is the letter F worth three points, four points or five points?	*Four points*
7 Which English soccer club are nicknamed "The Villains"?	*Aston Villa*
8 What 5 letter P word is the name given to the prize money for a boxing bout?	*The purse*
9 How many minutes does each half last in a game of soccer?	*45*
10 In the World Wrestling Entertainment, which wrestler is the brother of "The Undertaker"?	*Kane*

Quiz 127
Question 5

Quiz 127

For the Little Leaguers

Questions	Answers
1 In which country did Kung fu originate?	*China*
2 Which U.S. tennis star married Steffi Graff?	*Andre Agassi*
3 Which sport is played at Twickenham?	*Rugby Union*
4 What is the most valuable ball in the game of snooker?	*Black ball (worth seven)*
5 In which sport are there categories of tantamweight, flyweight or featherweight?	*Boxing*
6 In soccer, can a goal be scored directly from a corner kick?	*Yes*
7 What nationality is Michael Schumacher?	*German*
8 Which club did Dennis Wise captain to win the FA Cup?	*Chelsea*
9 In which sport is the small target ball called the jack?	*Bowls*
10 In volleyball, what is the maximum number of times a team can touch the ball before it crosses the net?	*Three*

Quiz 128
Question 8

Quiz 128
Question 4

Quiz 130
A Sports Bag

Questions	Answers
1 Which snooker player won TV's first *Pot Black* series?	*Ray Reardon*
2 What S word is the name given to the pace setter in a rowing team?	*The stroke*
3 In which sport is the Stella Artois Tournament contested?	*Tennis*
4 Which Scottish born jockey's Derby winners include Troy and Henbit?	*Willie Carson*
5 Which race was first contested in June 1846, from Henley Bridge to Hambledon Lock?	*The Oxford and Cambridge boat race*
6 Who was crowned Darts World Champion on five occasions in the 1980s?	*Eric Bristow*
7 Which Italian Serie A soccer club play their home matches in the town of Bergamo?	*Atalanta*
8 Sapporo was the first city to host the Winter Olympics. In which country is it?	*Japan*
9 What kind of animal is Ballyregan Bob who won a record 32 consecutive races?	*A greyhound*
10 What number is directly opposite the number six on a dartboard?	*11*

Quiz 129
Question 6

Quiz 129

A Sports Bag

Questions	Answers
1 Which horse won the 2006 Grand National?	*Numbersixvalverde*
2 In horseracing, which course official is known by the initials COTC?	*Clerk Of The Course*
3 Who moved to the New York Yankees from the Boston Red Sox in 1921 for a fee of $125,000?	*Babe Ruth*
4 Who was World Professional Billiards Champion from 1968 to 1980?	*Rex Williams*
5 In which city did Allan Wells win an Olympic gold medal?	*Moscow*
6 Who was ranked as Britain's No. 1 male tennis player in 2001?	*Tim Henman*
7 From which wood were longbows traditionally made?	*Yew*
8 What B word is the name of a form of hockey played on ice with a ball?	*Bandy*
9 Who was the first South African golfer to win the U.S. Open?	*Gary Player*
10 What is the highest possible dan in judo?	*12th dan*

Quiz 132
The 2002 World Cup

Questions	Answers
1 Who, surprisingly, won the first game of the competition, beating the defending champions France?	Senegal
2 Who scored Brazil's winning goal against England and was later shown a red card in the same game?	Ronaldinho
3 How many nations competed in the 2002 World Cup finals?	Thirty-two
4 Which player, on the books of Manchester United, scored for South Africa?	Quentin Fortune
5 Which Brazilian was fined for feigning injury in their group game against Turkey?	Rivaldo
6 Who knocked Ireland out of the tournament in a penalty shoot out?	Spain
7 For which European nation did Pauleta grab a hat trick?	Portugal
8 Who scored England's only penalty in the tournament?	David Beckham
9 Which nation finished fourth in the 2002 World Cup?	South Korea
10 Who scored an injury time equaliser for Ireland against Germany?	Robbie Keane

Quiz 131
Question 10

Quiz 131
Question 6

Quiz 131
The 2002 World Cup

Questions	Answers
1 Who scored England's first goal in the tournament?	*Sol Campbell*
2 Who was the oldest outfield player in England's 2002 World Cup squad?	*Martin Keown*
3 What is the four-letter name of the player who captained the winners of the tournament?	*Cafu*
4 Who scored the winning goal for Germany in the semi-final, and was banned from playing in the final?	*Michael Ballack*
5 Which striker scored a hat trick for Germany against Saudi Arabia?	*Miroslav Klose*
6 Who was the youngest player in England's World Cup squad?	*Joe Cole*
7 Which nation won the third place play-off?	*Turkey*
8 Who, with eight goals, finished as the leading scorer in the tournament?	*Ronaldo*
9 In which city was the 2002 World Cup final played?	*Yokohama*
10 Guus Hiddink was the manager of which of the host nations?	*South Korea*

Quiz 132
Question 2

Quiz 134
A Sports Bag

Questions	Answers
1 Which country does athlete Liz McColgan come from?	*Scotland*
2 For which swimming stroke did Duncan Goodhew win an Olympic gold medal?	*Breaststroke*
3 What country did Kapil Dev play test cricket for?	*India*
4 For which European nation did Christian Vieri play?	*Italy*
5 What is the national sport of Spain?	*Bullfighting*
6 Who scored two goals for France in the 1998 World Cup final against Brazil?	*Zinedine Zidane*
7 Which former snooker World Champion is nicknamed "The Nugget"?	*Steve Davis*
8 In which sport do teams compete for the Harry Sunderland Trophy?	*Rugby league*
9 How many zones are there on an archery target?	*Ten*
10 Which soccer team lost three FA Cup finals in the 1980s?	*Everton*

Quiz 133
Question 1

Quiz 133
Question 9

Quiz 133
A Sports Bag

Questions	Answers
1 What is the nationality of tennis star Lleyton Hewitt?	*Australian*
2 Which skater won an Olympic gold for Britain in 1976?	*John Curry*
3 Who were England's first opponents in the 2006 World Cup finals?	*Paraguay*
4 Which swimming stroke made its Olympic debut in 1956?	*Butterfly*
5 Which tennis star, nicknamed "Little Mo", was the first woman to win the Grand Slam?	*Maureen Connolly*
6 What is the most popular indoor sport in the United States?	*Basketball*
7 Who was the first footballer to score 100 goals in England's Premiership?	*Alan Shearer*
8 Which member of The Monkees pop group was a former apprentice jockey?	*Davy Jones*
9 From which country does the mother of Tiger Woods hail?	*Thailand*
10 What soccer club was Brian Clough managing when he announced his retirement from the game?	*Nottingham Forest*

Quiz 134
Question 6

Quiz 136
A Sports Bag

Questions	Answers
1 Including the cue ball, how many balls are on a snooker table at the start of play?	*22*
2 On what type of surface is the French Open tennis tournament played?	*Clay*
3 Who was sent off in a 1986 World Cup match, whilst captaining England?	*Ray Wilkins*
4 Which American motor race was first held in 1911?	*Indianapolis 500*
5 Were substitutes first allowed in soccer's World Cup in 1962, 1966 or 1970?	*1970*
6 At which winter Olympic venue did Eddie the Eagle Edwards represent Britain at ski jumping?	*Calgary*
7 Who did Brazil beat in the final when winning the World Cup for the first time in 1958?	*Sweden*
8 In which sport are prime and octave both the names of defensive positions?	*Fencing*
9 Which Italian soccer referee, nicknamed "The Skull", took charge of the 2002 World Cup final?	*Pierluigi Collina*
10 On which island are the motorcycle TT Races held?	*Isle Of Man*

Quiz 135
Question 2

Quiz 135
A Sports Bag

Questions	Answers
1 Who founded the Matchroom Snooker Organisation?	*Barry Hearn*
2 At which sport did Suzanne Dando represent Great Britain?	*Gymnastics*
3 In 2005, the San Antonio Spurs won their third championship title in seven years in which sport?	*Basketball*
4 What boxing weight category comes between bantamweight and lightweight?	*Featherweight*
5 What type of wood are hurling sticks made from, is it willow, ash or yew?	*Ash*
6 Which Olympic gold medallist of 1968 went on to become World Heavyweight Boxing Champion?	*George Foreman*
7 Who worked as a sports commentator before becoming President of the United States?	*Ronald Reagan*
8 Which was the first British club that Eric Cantona played for?	*Leeds United*
9 What sport is played by the New Jersey Devils?	*Ice hockey*
10 Who was England's manager in the 1990 soccer World Cup?	*Bobby Robson*

Quiz 136
Question 6

Quiz 138
Track Trivia & Field Facts

Questions	Answers
1 Which track race is contested over 25 laps of the track?	*10,000 m*
2 Who was the first British track athlete to win two gold medals at the World Athletics Championships?	*Colin Jackson*
3 Who became the fastest man on Earth when he ran 9.78 seconds for the 100 m in September 2002?	*Tim Montgomery*
4 Western roll, Fosbury Flop and straddle are all styles of what?	*High jump*
5 Which British athlete won a 400 m silver medal at the 1996 Olympic games?	*Roger Black*
6 Which Cuban athlete, born in 1950, was nicknamed "White Lightning"?	*Alberto Juantorena*
7 Which British athlete was disqualified from the 1996 Olympic 100 m final for two false starts?	*Linford Christie*
8 At the 2004 Athens Olympics, which Jamaican sprinter set a new world record for the men's 100 m?	*Asafa Powell*
9 Founded in 1880, what do the initials AAA stand for?	*Amateur Athletics Association*
10 From 1983 to 1997, who won six gold medals for the pole vault at the World Athletics Championships?	*Sergey Bubka*

Quiz 137
Question 9

Quiz 137

Track Trivia & Field Facts

Questions	Answers
1 In which athletic event do competitors employ the O'Brien Shift?	*Shot putt*
2 In 1988, who became the first Olympic gold medallist to be disqualified?	*Ben Johnson*
3 What is the only object that is thrown in the women's heptathlon?	*The javelin*
4 How many summer Olympics were held in Africa in the 20th century?	*None*
5 Over what distance did Sebastian Coe win two Olympic gold medals?	*1500 m*
6 Which country did Cathy Freeman represent at the 2000 Olympics?	*Australia*
7 In 1999, which American was voted Male Athlete of the Century by the IAAF?	*Carl Lewis*
8 Who won a 200 m silver medal for Britain at the 2000 Olympics?	*Darren Campbell*
9 Which obstacles in athletics stand 106.7 cm high?	*The hurdles in men's 110 m races*
10 Who was the first athlete to jump in excess of 18 m in the triple jump?	*Jonathan Edwards*

Quiz 138
Question 7

Quiz 140

Total Trivia

Questions	Answers
1 At the 1956 Melbourne Olympics, why were the equestrian events held in Stockholm?	*Due to quarantine laws*
2 From which mountain did Ashley Doubtfire set a high descent hang gliding record in 1979?	*Mount Kilimanjaro*
3 In Judo, what is an *ippon*?	*A winning point*
4 Was Joseph Filliston 10 or 100 when he umpired a Lords Taverners versus Old England match at Lords?	*100 years old*
5 What is the only event in which India won an Olympic gold medal in the 20th century?	*Hockey*
6 Which wicket keeper notched a record 355 test dismissals in his 14-year career representing Australia?	*Rodney Marsh*
7 Which footballer was the only player to score a hat-trick against Peter Shilton in his 125 England games?	*Marco Van Basten*
8 Which car manufacturer was the first to record 100 Grand Prix wins in Formula One?	*Ferrari*
9 1970 was the first year in which 100 competitors finished which sporting race?	*Tour de France*
10 In which sport do the 70 winning moves include twists, shoves and flips?	*Sumo wrestling*

Quiz 139
Question 7

Quiz 139

Total Trivia

Questions	Answers
1 Which city hosted the 2005 World Athletics Championships?	Helsinki
2 Which track star beat a racehorse over a sprint course in 1936?	Jesse Owens
3 In the 1920s, which legendary Everton striker scored 60 goals in a single season including seven hat-tricks?	Dixie Dean
4 How old was Lester Piggott when he rode his first winner, was he 12 or 13?	12
5 Who was the first person to fly solo around the world in a hot air balloon?	Steve Fossett
6 Who took 19 wickets in two innings in a 1956 cricket test match between England and Australia?	Jim Laker
7 Which was the first motorcycle manufacturer to register 400 Grand Prix wins?	Yamaha
8 In which sport has Victor Barna won 15 world titles?	Table tennis
9 In 1875, Aristides became the first winner of which race?	The Kentucky Derby
10 Which British rower won his fifth successive Olympic gold medal at the Sydney Games?	Steve Redgrave

Quiz 140
Question 8

Quiz 142
A Sports Bag

Questions	Answers
1 Which former Wimbledon champion wrote his autobiography entitled *Serious*?	*John McEnroe*
2 Who is the only English footballer to have scored two goals in a 20th century European Cup final?	*Bobby Charlton*
3 What was the name of the speedboat in which Donald Campbell died?	Bluebird
4 In which Japanese city did England beat Argentina 1-0 in the 2002 World Cup?	*Sapporo*
5 Who won the men's singles at Wimbledon in 1992 and won an Olympic gold medal four years later?	*Andre Agassi*
6 Which Australian entrepreneur established his World Cricket Circus in 1977?	*Kerry Packer*
7 What sporting object has 82 separate scoring zones?	*A dartboard*
8 Standard Liege soccer club hail from which European country?	*Belgium*
9 What is the name of the trophy presented to the winner of the women's singles at Wimbledon?	*The Rosewater Dish*
10 Who scored the winning goal for Real Madrid in the 2002 European Cup final?	*Zinedine Zidane*

Quiz 141
Question 1

Quiz 141
A Sports Bag

Questions	Answers
1 Who was the first Dutchman to win the men's singles at Wimbledon?	*Richard Krajicek*
2 In 2005, which American was named Sportsman of the Year by Sports Illustrated Magazine?	*Lance Armstrong*
3 In which New Zealand city is the cricket test ground, Eden Park?	*Auckland*
4 Who was the last British female tennis player in the 20th century to be ranked in the world's top ten?	*Sue Barker*
5 In which sport do competitors wear a protective arm pad called a bracer?	*Archery*
6 What shape is the area in which a sumo wrestling bout is fought?	*Round*
7 Where would you play the game Baccarat?	*In a casino*
8 Soccer manager, Alex Ferguson, owns a racehorse called what?	*Rock of Gibraltar*
9 During exercise, which acid builds up in the muscles?	*Lactic acid*
10 What is the nickname of Darlington F.C.?	*"The Quakers"*

Quiz 142
Question 1

Quiz 144
A Trivia Vault

Questions	Answers
1 Which Russian gymnast was named Female Athlete of the Year 1972?	*Olga Korbut*
2 On what piece of apparatus do women perform the Hecht manoeuvre?	*Asymmetric bars*
3 What nationality is the Olympic gymnast, Shannon Miller?	*American*
4 Where are a *yamashita* and a *yurchenko* performed?	*On the vaulting horse*
5 Which Romanian gymnast won three gold medals at the 1976 Olympics?	*Nadia Comaneci*
6 Which Russian, who won five Olympic golds, was born in 1957, to a Korean father and Mongolian mother?	*Nellie Kim*
7 The pig is the alternative name for which piece of gymnastic apparatus?	*Pommel horse*
8 Did the Russian gymnast Larisa Latynina win 15, 16 or 17 Olympic medals in her career?	*17: 9 gold, 5 silver and 3 bronze*
9 In gymnastics, what is 5 m long and 10 cm wide?	*The women's beam*
10 Did the U.S. gymnasts win any gold medals at the Sydney Olympics?	*No*

Quiz 143
Question 2

Quiz 143
A Trivia Vault

Questions	Answers
1 How is the world governing body for gymnastics known for short?	*FIG*
2 Which form of gymnastics involves the use of hand apparatus such as ribbons, balls and hoops?	*Rhythmic gymnastics*
3 Which apparatus in men's gymnastics stands 195 cm from the floor?	*Parallel bars*
4 Which nation won the most Olympic team championships in the 20th century?	*U.S.S.R.*
5 What is a perfect score in a gymnastic exercise?	*Ten*
6 Other than the vault, what is the only gymnastic exercise in which both men and women compete?	*The floor*
7 What nationality is the gymnast Yukio Endo?	*Japanese*
8 True or false? Gymnastic events were contested in the very first Modern Olympics of 1896.	*True*
9 On what type of horse do men perform a manoeuvre called the double leg circle?	*Pommel horse*
10 What is the nickname of the Ukraine gymnast Lilia Podkapayevo?	*"Lilipod"*

Quiz 144
Question 9

Quiz 146
A Sports Bag

Questions	Answers
1 In Olympic field events, which projectile is thrown by men only?	*The hammer*
2 Which boxer became World Heavyweight Champion in 1994, at the age of 45?	*George Foreman*
3 Which Midlands club won the FA Cup for the first time in their history in 1987?	*Coventry City*
4 In what game would you use a shot called a boast?	*Squash*
5 In which U.S. city was the tennis star Jennifer Capriati born?	*New York*
6 Who captained the England soccer team on 65 occasions between 1982 and 1991?	*Bryan Robson*
7 Which arm does a cricket umpire raise to indicate a no ball?	*The right arm*
8 What is the more common name for a natatorium?	*Swimming pool*
9 Who was the winning horse of the 1992 Grand National, the year of a General Election?	*Party Politics*
10 Where were the 1940 Olympics scheduled to be held before the intervention of World War II?	*London*

Quiz 145
Question 5

Quiz 145
A Sports Bag

Questions	Answers
1 In 1981, professional league soccer was played in Britain for the first time on what day?	*Sunday*
2 Which ball sport was originally called baggataway?	*Lacrosse*
3 In baseball, what is the name given to a player who can bat with either hand?	*A switch–hitter*
4 Which boss of Middlesbrough was a member of England's coaching staff at the 2002 World Cup?	*Steve McClaren*
5 Who were Mick The Miller and Patricia's Hope?	*Greyhounds*
6 What nationality did the tennis star Hana Mandlikova adopt after leaving Czechoslovakia?	*Australian*
7 What is the only Olympic sailing class for a three-man crew?	*Soling*
8 In which year was the London Marathon first contested?	*1981*
9 Which former Pakistan cricket captain married Jemima Goldsmith?	*Imran Khan*
10 What kind of animal is Yorkie, the official mascot of York City F.C.?	*A lion*

Quiz 146
Question 8

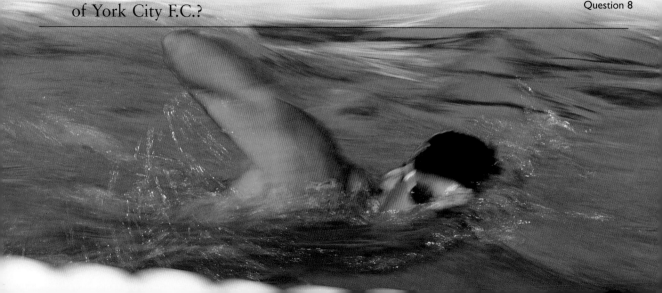

For the Little Leaguers

Questions	Answers
1 In which sport is the ball slam dunked through a raised hoop?	*Basketball*
2 In cricket, what do the letters c & b signify?	*Caught and bowled*
3 Which female WWF star is nicknamed "The Ninth Wonder Of The World"?	*Chyna*
4 What is worth 50 points on a dartboard?	*The bull's-eye*
5 In the game of golf, is an eagle or a birdie the better score?	*An eagle*
6 For which country are Nicolas Anelka and Patrick Vieira team mates?	*France*
7 In what word game is part of a gallows drawn for every wrong answer given?	*Hangman*
8 How many balls are worth more than one point in a game of snooker?	*Six*
9 Which is the only British professional soccer team containing the letter J in its name?	*St. Johnstone*
10 Which rower was voted BBC Sports Personality of the Year in 2000?	*Steve Redgrave*

Quiz 147
Question 7

Quiz 147

For the Little Leaguers

Questions	Answers
1 In which sport do competitors try to play below par?	*Golf*
2 What do the letters OG stand for in a game of soccer?	*Own goal*
3 Players in which sport throw projectiles from behind the oche?	*Darts*
4 Which WWF wrestler and commentator is nicknamed "The King"?	*Jerry Lawler*
5 Which Scottish soccer club has a five-letter name beginning with C, which is also a boy's first name?	*Clyde*
6 What is the title of the TV game show with Gary Lineker and David Gower as team captains?	**They Think It's All Over**
7 What is the ball hit with in a game of volleyball?	*The hands*
8 How many cox take part in the Oxford and Cambridge Boat Race?	*Two, one for each crew*
9 Who contests the Ashes cricket trophy with England?	*Australia*
10 Which is the only English Football League team beginning with the letter I?	*Ipswich Town*

Quiz 148
Question 1

Quiz 150
Sport On Wheels

Questions	Answers
1 What are cyclists doing if they are honking?	*Standing out of their saddles*
2 In which U.S. state is The Daytona 500 motor race staged?	*Florida*
3 What was the nationality of the first Formula One World Champion?	*Italian (Guiseppe Farina)*
4 Which American rider was World Speedway Champion in 1982?	*Bruce Penhall*
5 Which Austrian driver, nicknamed "The Computer", came back to racing after a horrific crash in 1976?	*Niki Lauda*
6 Which Texan cyclist won the 1999 Tour de France?	*Lance Armstrong*
7 In which Brazilian city is the Interlagos Grand Prix circuit?	*Rio de Janeiro*
8 Fernando Alonso was the first driver from which country to be crowned Formula One Champion?	*Spain*
9 In cycling, where is the San Sebastian Classic contested?	*Spain*
10 Which track staged the 2002 British Grand Prix in Formula One?	*Silverstone*

Quiz 149
Question 6

Quiz 149
Sport On Wheels

Questions	Answers
1 In which country was the speedway legend Ivan Mauger born?	*New Zealand*
2 For which racing team did Nigel Mansell win the Formula One World Championship in 1992?	*Williams*
3 Who was the first Irish man to win the Tour de France?	*Stephen Roche*
4 In which desert did Margaret Thatcher's son Mark lose his way in a 1982 car rally?	*Sahara Desert*
5 In which city is the Catalunya Montjuich Grand Prix circuit?	*Barcelona*
6 What is the alternative name for motocross?	*Scrambling*
7 Which company's tyres did the Ferrari Formula One team use in 2001?	*Bridgestone*
8 In which country does the cycle race, called The Tour of Lombardy, take place?	*Italy*
9 In 1975, who was the first woman to drive in a Formula One race?	*Lella Lombardi*
10 Which motor racing driver was born in the Scottish town of Twynholm in 1971?	*David Coulthard*

Quiz 150
Question 5

Questions	Answers
1 In which Olympic sport are all the men's events contested over a distance of 2000 m?	*Rowing*
2 In archery, what do the initials GMB stand for?	*Grand Master Bowman*
3 What sporting projectile for women weighs 600 gm and has a minimum length of 220 cm?	*The javelin*
4 What is the name of Gary and Phil Neville's father?	*Neville Neville*
5 In which sport does the egg position increase a competitors speed?	*Skiing*
6 In 2001 who became the first American football team with a bird name to win the Super Bowl?	*Baltimore Ravens*
7 Which sporting body has the initials EWCB?	*England and Wales Cricket Board*
8 What is the shorter name for the British Isles Rugby Union team?	*British Lions*
9 In which martial art is a drawn match called a *hikiwake*?	*Kendo*
10 In which sport is the end puller called "The Anchor"?	*Tug of War*

Quiz 152
Question 3

Quiz 152
Question 4